LITTLE PUFFERS

A Guide to Britain's Narrow Gauge Railways 2014-2015

EDITOR
John Robinson

Tenth Edition

RAILWAY LOCATOR MAP

The numbers shown on this map relate to the page numbers for each railway. Pages 5-6 contain an alphabetical listing of the railways featured in this guide. Please note that the markers on this map show the approximate location only.

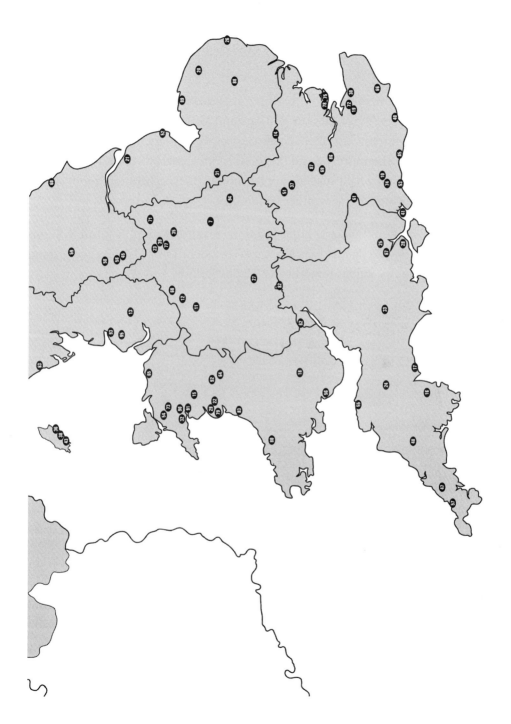

ACKNOWLEDGEMENTS

We were greatly impressed by the friendly and cooperative manner of the staff and helpers of the railways which we selected to appear in this book, and wish to thank them all for the help they have given. In addition we wish to thank Bob Budd (cover design), Michael Robinson (page layouts) and Jonathan James (who provided a number of photographs) for their help.

Although we believe that the information contained in this guide is accurate at the time of going to press, we, and the Railways and Museums itemised, are unable to accept liability for any loss, damage, distress or injury suffered as a result of any inaccuracies. Furthermore, we and the Railways are unable to guarantee operating and opening times which may always be subject to cancellation without notice, particularly during adverse weather conditions.

If you feel we should include other locations or information in future editions, please let us know so that we may give them consideration. We would like to thank you for buying this guide and wish you 'Happy Railway Travelling'!

John Robinson
EDITOR

British Library Cataloguing in Publication Data
A catalogue record for this book is available from the British Library

ISBN-13:   978-1-86223-292-1

Copyright © 2014, MARKSMAN PUBLICATIONS. (01472 696226)
72 St. Peter's Avenue, Cleethorpes, N.E. Lincolnshire, DN35 8HU, England

Manufactured in the UK by Ashford Colour Press Ltd.

FOREWORD

For the purposes of this publication, we define railways solely by their gauge and include only those with a gauge in excess of 7¼ inches but less than UK Standard gauge. We also publish 'Still Steaming', a separate guide for Standard gauge railways and 'Tiny Trains', a guide for railways with gauges of 7¼ inches and smaller. Both of these guides, as well as further copies of 'Little Puffers' can be ordered UK post free from the Marksman Publications address opposite.

The cover photograph was provided by the Amberley Museum and Heritage Centre and shows their locomotive 'Peter' pulling a Santa Special into Cragside Station.

CONTENTS

ABBEY PUMPING STATION

Address: Abbey Pumping Station Museum, Corporation Road, Leicester, LE4 5PX	**Nº of Steam Locos**: 1
Telephone Nº: (0116) 299-5113	**Nº of Other Locos**: 4
Year Formed: 1980s	**Nº of Members**: Approximately 140
Location of Line: Leicester	**Annual Membership Fee**: £8.00 Adult
Length of Line: 300 yards	**Approx Nº of Visitors P.A.**: 60,000
	Gauge: 2 feet
	Web site: www.abbeypumpingstation.org

GENERAL INFORMATION

Nearest Mainline Station: Leicester London Road (3 miles)
Nearest Bus Station: Leicester (1½ miles)
Car Parking: Free parking available on site (Free parking at the Space Centre on Special Event days)
Coach Parking: Use the Space Centre car park
Souvenir Shop(s): Yes
Food & Drinks: Available on special event days only

SPECIAL INFORMATION

The Museum is situated in the Abbey Pumping Station which, from 1891 to 1964 pumped Leicester's sewage to nearby treatment works. The Museum now collects and displays the industrial, technological and scientific heritage of Leicester and contains rare working examples of Woolf compound rotative beam engines which are in steam on selected days.

OPERATING INFORMATION

Opening Times: The Pumping Station is open daily from February to October, 11.00am to 4.30pm. Trains run on the dates detailed below.
Steam Working: Selected Special Event days only: 2014 dates: 13th April; 3rd May; 7th, 28th & 29th June; 5th July; 7th September; 4th October; 7th December; 11th January 2015; 1st February 2015.
Prices: Adults £3.50 (Special event days only)
Concessions £2.50 (Special events only)
Family £8.00 (Special event days only)

Detailed Directions by Car:
From All Parts: The Museum is situated next to the National Space Centre, about 1 mile North of Leicester city centre near Beaumont Leys and Belgrave. Brown tourist signs with a distinctive rocket logo provide directions to the NSC from the arterial routes around Leicester and the Museum is nearby.

ALFORD VALLEY RAILWAY

Address: Alford Station, Main Street, Alford, Aberdeenshire   AB33 8HH
Telephone Nº: (07879) 293934
Year Formed: 1979
Location of Line: Alford – Haughton Park
Length of Line: 1 mile

Nº of Steam Locos: None at present
Nº of Other Locos: 3
Approx Nº of Visitors P.A.: 12,000
Gauge: 2 feet
Web site: www.alfordvalleyrailway.org.uk
E-mail: info@alfordvalleyrailway.org.uk

GENERAL INFORMATION

Nearest Mainline Station: Insch (10 miles)
Nearest Bus Station: Alford (200 yards)
Car Parking: Available on site
Coach Parking: Available on site
Souvenir Shop(s): Yes
Food & Drinks: The railway hopes to be able to provide refreshments during 2014.

SPECIAL INFORMATION

The Grampian Transport Museum is adjacent to the Railway and the Heritage Centre also has horse-drawn tractors and agricultural machinery.

OPERATING INFORMATION

Opening Times: 2014 dates: Saturdays, Sundays and Bank Holiday Mondays in April, May, June and September. Open daily during July and August. Trains usually run from 12.30pm to 4.00pm. Santa Specials operate during the first two weekends in December when higher fares apply.
Steam Working: None at present
Prices: Adult Return £4.50
　　　　　Child Return £3.50
　　　　　Family 'Weekly Pass' £20.00
　　　　　Season Ticket £35.00

Detailed Directions by Car:
From All Parts: Alford is situated 25 miles west of Aberdeen on the Highland tourist route. Take the A944 to reach Alford.

ALMOND VALLEY LIGHT RAILWAY

Address: Almond Valley Heritage Centre, Millfield, Livingston   EH54 7AR
Telephone Nº: (01506) 414957
Year Formed: 1993
Location of Line: Livingston
Length of Line: 550 yards

Nº of Steam Locos: None
Nº of Other Locos: 3
Approx Nº of Visitors P.A.: 125,000
Gauge: 2 feet 6 inches
Web site: www.almondvalley.co.uk
E-mail: rac@almondvalley.co.uk

GENERAL INFORMATION

Nearest Mainline Station: Livingston North (1 mile)
Nearest Bus Station: Livingston (1 mile)
Car Parking: Available on site
Coach Parking: Available
Souvenir Shop(s): Yes
Food & Drinks: Available

SPECIAL INFORMATION

The railway runs through the grounds of the Almond Valley Heritage Centre which hosts a wide range of other attractions including a farm, a historic Mill, nature trails and picnic areas.

OPERATING INFORMATION

Opening Times: The Centre is open daily throughout the year but for 25th & 26th December and 1st & 2nd January. The railway operates at weekends between Easter and the end of September, and daily during some holiday periods, from 11.00am to 4.00pm. Please contact Almond Valley for further details.
Steam Working: None at present.
Prices: Adults £6.50 (Admission to Centre)
        Children £5.00 (Admission to Centre)
        Family £19.00 (Admission to Centre)
Note: Train rides are an extra £1.00 per person.

Detailed Directions by Car:
From All Parts: Exit the M8 at Junction 3A and take the A779 towards Livingston. Almond Valley Heritage Centre is located near the junction of the A779 and the A705 and is clearly signposted.

AMBERLEY MUSEUM & HERITAGE CENTRE

Address: Amberley Museum & Heritage Centre, Amberley, Arundel   BN18 9LT
Telephone Nº: (01798) 831370
E-mail: office@amberleymuseum.co.uk
Year Formed: 1979
Location of Line: Amberley
Length of Line: ¾ mile

Nº of Steam Locos: 3
Nº of Other Locos: 20+
Nº of Members: 300 volunteers
Annual Membership Fee: £22.00
Approx Nº of Visitors P.A.: 60,000
Gauge: 2 feet
Web site: www.amberleymuseum.co.uk

GENERAL INFORMATION

Nearest Mainline Station: Amberley (adjacent)
Nearest Bus Station: –
Car Parking: Free parking available on site
Coach Parking: Free parking available on site
Souvenir Shop(s): Yes
Food & Drinks: Yes

SPECIAL INFORMATION

Amberley Museum covers 36 acres of former chalk pits and comprises over 30 buildings containing hundreds of different exhibits.

OPERATING INFORMATION

Opening Times: 2014 dates: Wednesday to Sunday from 12th March to 2nd November and also on Bank Holiday Mondays. Open daily in August and during other local School Holidays. Trains operate from 11.00am until 4.00pm
Steam Working: Please phone for details.
Prices: Adult £11.00
        Child £6.60 (free for Under-4's)
        Concessions £10.00
        Family £32.00 (2 adults + 3 children)

Detailed Directions by Car:
From All Parts: Amberley Museum is situated in West Sussex on the B2139 mid-way between Arundel and Storrington and is adjacent to Amberley Railway Station.

AMERTON RAILWAY

Address: Amerton Farm, Stow-by-Chartley, Staffordshire ST18 0LA
Telephone N°: (01785) 850965
Year Formed: 1991
Location: Amerton Farm
Length of Line: Approximately 1 mile

N° of Steam Locos: 3 (+2 in restoration)
N° of Other Locos: 7 (+2 in restoration)
N° of Members: 60
Approx N° of Visitors P.A.: 30,000
Gauge: 2 feet
Web site: www.amertonrailway.co.uk

GENERAL INFORMATION

Nearest Mainline Station: Stafford (8 miles)
Nearest Bus Station: Stafford (8 miles)
Car Parking: Free parking available on site
Coach Parking: Available by arrangement
Souvenir Shop(s): Yes
Food & Drinks: Yes

SPECIAL INFORMATION

The Railway is run by volunteers and the circuit was completed in 2002. The Summer Steam Gala in 2014 will be held on 14th & 15th June.

OPERATING INFORMATION

Opening Times: 2014 dates: Weekends from the 22nd March to 2nd November and daily during the School Holidays. Santa Specials run on weekends from 29th November to 21st December. Open from 11.30am to 4.30pm at weekends but only until 4.00pm during midweek dates.
Steam Working: Sundays and Bank Holidays plus some other Special Events. Please contact the railway for further information.
Prices: Adult £2.20   Child £1.50
Concession £1.70
E-mail: enquiries@amertonrailway.co.uk

Detailed Directions by Car:
Amerton is located on the A518, 1 mile from the junction with the A51 – Amerton Farm is signposted at the junction. The Railway is located approximately 8 miles from Junction 14 of the M6.

APEDALE VALLEY LIGHT RAILWAY

Address: Apedale Valley Country Park, Chesterton, Newcastle Under Lyme
Telephone Nº: 0845 484950
Year Formed: 1969
Location: Apedale Valley Country Park
Length of Line: ¼ mile

Nº of Steam Locos: 3
Nº of Other Locos: 67
Nº of Members: 200+
Annual Membership Fee: £17.00
Gauge: 2 feet
Web site: www.avlr.org.uk

GENERAL INFORMATION

Nearest Mainline Station: Longport (2 miles)
Nearest Bus Station: Hanley (3½ miles)
Car Parking: Available
Coach Parking: Available
Souvenir Shop(s): Yes
Food & Drinks: Available

SPECIAL INFORMATION

The Apedale Valley Light Railway is operated by the Moseley Railway Trust (www.mrt.org.uk).

OPERATING INFORMATION

Opening Times: 2014 dates: Saturdays and some Sundays from 12th April to 26th October. Santa Specials run on some weekends in December. Trains usually run from 11.30am to 4.00pm. Please contact the railway for further information.
Steam Working: Bank Holiday Sundays and Mondays plus the second weekend in each month from April to October inclusive.
Prices: Adult £2.50
Child £1.50
Note: Different prices may apply for special events.

Detailed Directions by Car:
Exit the M6 at Junction 16 and take the A500 to the A34 and head southwards. Turn right at the traffic island by the McDonald's restaurant and follow the brown tourist signs for Apedale Valley. Follow Loomer Road in Chesterton to the end and continue into the Park. Use the car park at the Heritage Centre as there is no direct access to the railway by car. SatNav: Use ST5 7LB. This postcode is the speedway track on the approach to the park. Continue past the speedway track and continue along Loomer Road for the park.

ASTLEY GREEN COLLIERY MUSEUM

Address: Higher Green Lane,
Astley Green, Tyldesley   M29 7JB
Telephone Nº: (01942) 708969
Year Formed: 1983
Location of Line: Astley Green Colliery
Length of Line: 440 yards

Nº of Steam Locos: None
Nº of Other Locos: 33
Nº of Members: 120
Approx Nº of Visitors P.A.: 6,000
Gauge: 2 feet
Web site: www.agcm.org.uk

GENERAL INFORMATION

Nearest Mainline Station: Salford (3 miles)
Nearest Bus Station: Manchester (5 miles)
Car Parking: Available on site
Coach Parking: Available
Souvenir Shop(s): None
Food & Drinks: None

SPECIAL INFORMATION

Astley Green Colliery Museum houses the largest
collection of underground colliery locos in the UK.
The 440 yard line is used for freight demonstrations.

OPERATING INFORMATION

Opening Times: Tuesday, Thursday, Saturday and
Sunday throughout the year except for Christmas
Day and Boxing Day. Also open at other times by
prior arrangement. Open from 1.30pm to 5.00pm.
Steam Working: None
Prices: No admission charge but donations are
gratefully accepted.
Note: The museum does not offer passenger rides.

Detailed Directions by Car:
From All Parts: Exit the M6 at Junction 23 and take the A580 towards Manchester. After about 6 miles cross the
Bridgewater Canal then take the next right signposted Higher Green. After approximately ¼ mile turn left into
the Colliery grounds.

AUDLEY END STEAM RAILWAY

Address: Audley End, Saffron Walden, Essex	**Length of Line:** 1½ miles
Telephone Nº: (01799) 542134	**Nº of Steam Locos:** 5
Year Formed: 1964	**Nº of Other Locos:** 2
Location of Line: Opposite Audley End House, Saffron Walden	**Approx Nº of Visitors P.A.:** 42,000
	Gauge: 10¼ inches
	Web site: www.audley-end-railway.co.uk

GENERAL INFORMATION

Nearest Mainline Station: Audley End (1 mile)
Nearest Bus Station: Saffron Walden (1 mile)
Car Parking: Available on site
Coach Parking: Available on site
Souvenir Shop(s): Yes
Food & Drinks: Snacks available

SPECIAL INFORMATION

Audley End Steam Railway is Lord Braybrooke's private miniature railway situated just next to Audley End House, an English Heritage site. Private parties can be catered for outside of normal running hours.

OPERATING INFORMATION

Opening Times: 2014 dates: Weekends and Bank Holidays from 29th March to 31st October and also daily during the School Holidays. Santa Specials operate on 6th, 7th, 13th, 14th and 17th to 24th December. Trains run from 12.00pm (11.00am on Bank Holidays) until approximately 4.45pm.
Steam Working: Weekends and Bank Holidays.
Prices: Adult Return £5.00
Child Return £4.00
Santa Specials £6.50
Note: Multi-ride tickets are also available.

Detailed Directions by Car:
Exit the M11 at Junction 10 if southbound or Junction 9 if northbound and follow the signs for Audley End House. The railway is situated just across the road from Audley End House.

BALA LAKE RAILWAY

Address: Bala Lake Railway,
Llanuwchllyn, Gwynedd, LL23 7DD
Telephone Nº: (01678) 540666
Year Formed: 1972
Location of Line: Llanuwchllyn to Bala
Length of Line: 4½ miles

Nº of Steam Locos: 4   (all are not in
Nº of Other Locos: 3   working order)
Approx Nº of Visitors P.A.: 20,000
Gauge: 1 foot 11 five-eighth inches
Web site: www.bala-lake-railway.co.uk
E-mail: balalake@btconnect.com

GENERAL INFORMATION

Nearest Mainline Station: Wrexham (40 miles)
Nearest Bus Station: Wrexham (40 miles)
Car Parking: Adequate parking in Llanuwchllyn
Coach Parking: At Llanuwchllyn or in Bala Town Centre
Souvenir Shop(s): Yes
Food & Drinks: Yes – unlicensed!

SPECIAL INFORMATION

Bala Lake Railway is a narrow-gauge railway which follows 4½ miles of the former Ruabon to Barmouth G.W.R. line.

OPERATING INFORMATION

Opening Times: Easter until the end of September but closed on Mondays and Fridays (excepting Bank Holidays) in April, May, June and September. Also open on some dates during October.
Steam Working: All advertised services are steam hauled. Trains run from 11.15am to 4.00pm.
Prices: Adult Single £6.50;   Return £9.50
Child Single £2.00
Senior Citizen Return £9.00
Family Tickets (Return): £11.50 (1 Adult + 1 Child);
£23.00 (2 Adults + 2 Children).
Additional Children pay £2.50 each.
Under 5's and dogs travel free of charge!

Detailed Directions by Car:
From All Parts: The railway is situated off the A494 Bala to Dolgellau road which is accessible from the national motorways via the A5 or A55.

BICKINGTON STEAM RAILWAY

Address: Trago Mills Shopping & Leisure Centre, Stover, Devon   TQ12 6JB
Telephone Nº: (01626) 821111
Year Formed: 1988
Location of Line: Near the junction of A38 and A382
Length of Line: 1½ miles

Nº of Steam Locos: 4
Nº of Other Locos: 1
Approx Nº of Visitors P.A.: Not known
Gauge: 10¼ inches
Web site: freespace.virgin.net/hanson.mike/Tragorailway.htm

GENERAL INFORMATION

Nearest Mainline Station: Newton Abbott (3½ miles)
Nearest Bus Station: Newton Abbott
Car Parking: Free parking available on site
Coach Parking: Available on site
Souvenir Shop(s): Yes
Food & Drinks: Available adjacent to the Railway

SPECIAL INFORMATION

Bickington Steam Railway is part of the Trago Mills Shopping & Leisure Centre which occupies around 100 acres of rolling South Devon countryside. The site has numerous other attractions including, 'The Finest 00-gauge Model Railway in the UK'!

OPERATING INFORMATION

Opening Times: Monday to Saturday 11.00am to 5.00pm and Sundays 12.00pm to 4.00pm.
Steam Working: Most operating days but please contact the Railway for precise information.
Prices: £2.00 for a Day Rover Ticket

Detailed Directions by Car:
From All Parts: Take the M5 from Exeter to the A38 and head towards Plymouth. Exit at the junction with the A382 and follow the signs for 'Trago Mills'. The railway is situated on this road after about 1 mile.

BICTON WOODLAND RAILWAY

Address: Bicton Woodland Railway, Bicton Park Botanical Gardens, East Budleigh, Budleigh Salterton EX9 7OP	**Nº of Steam Locos:** None at present
	Nº of Other Locos: 3
	Nº of Members: 15,000
Telephone Nº: (01395) 568465	**Annual Membership Fee:** From £17.00
Year Formed: 1963	**Approx Nº of Visitors P.A.:** 300,000
Location of Line: Bicton Gardens	**Gauge:** 1 foot 6 inches
Length of Line: 1½ miles	**Web site:** www.bictongardens.co.uk

GENERAL INFORMATION

Nearest Railtrack Station: Exmouth (6 miles)
Nearest Bus Station: Exeter (14 miles)
Car Parking: Free parking at site
Coach Parking: Free parking at site
Souvenir Shop(s): Yes
Food & Drinks: Yes

SPECIAL INFORMATION

The railway runs through the grounds of Bicton Park Botanical Gardens which span over 60 acres. The railway is the only 18 inch gauge line in the UK.

OPERATING INFORMATION

Opening Times: Daily 10.00am to 6.00pm during the Summer and 10.00am to 5.00pm during the Winter. Closed on Christmas Day and Boxing Day.
Steam Working: None at present
Prices: Adult £8.95 (Entrance); £1.90 (Rides)
Child £6.95 (Entrance); £1.50 (Rides)
Concessions £7.95 (Entrance); £1.70 (Rides)

Detailed Directions by Car:
From All Parts: Exit the M5 motorway at Exeter services, Junction 30 and follow the brown tourist signs to Bicton Park.

BRECON MOUNTAIN RAILWAY

Address: Pant Station, Merthyr Tydfil, CF48 2UP	**Gauge**: 1 foot 11¾ inches
Telephone Nº: (01685) 722988	**Length of Line**: 5 miles
Year Formed: 1980	**Nº of Steam Locos**: 8
Location of Line: North of Merthyr Tydfil – 1 mile from the A465	**Nº of Other Locos**: 3
	Approx Nº of Visitors P.A.: 75,000
	Web: www.breconmountainrailway.co.uk

GENERAL INFORMATION

Nearest Mainline Station: Merthyr Tydfil (3 miles)
Nearest Bus Station: Merthyr Tydfil (3 miles)
Car Parking: Free parking available at Pant Station
Coach Parking: Free parking available at Pant Station
Souvenir Shop(s): Yes
Food & Drinks: Yes – including licensed Tea Rooms

SPECIAL INFORMATION

It is possible to take a break before the return journey at Pontsticill to have a picnic, take a forest walk or visit the lakeside snackbar and play area.

OPERATING INFORMATION

Opening Times: Weekends and Bank Holidays throughout the year and daily during School holidays. Daily from the start of April to the end of October but closed on some Mondays and Fridays in April, May, September and October. Open almost every day in December for Santa Specials. Trains typically run from 10.30am to 3.45pm and from 12.00pm to 3.00pm during off-peak times.
Steam Working: Most services are steam hauled.
Prices: Adults £12.00
       Children £6.00 (Ages 2 and under ride free)
       Senior Citizens £10.75
Note: Two children can travel for £5.00 each when accompanying a paying adult.

Detailed Directions by Car:
Exit the M4 at Junction 32 and take the A470 to Merthyr Tydfil. Go onto the A465 and follow the brown tourist signs for the railway.   SATNAV users should enter the following postcode: CF48 2DD

BREDGAR & WORMSHILL LIGHT RAILWAY

Address: The Warren, Bredgar, near Sittingbourne, Kent ME9 8AT	**Gauge:** 2 feet
Telephone Nº: (01622) 884254	**Nº of Steam Locos:** 10
Year Formed: 1972	**Nº of Other Locos:** 5
Location of Line: 1 mile south of Bredgar	**Approx Nº of Visitors P.A.:** 7,000
Length of Line: ¾ mile	**Web site:** www.bwlr.co.uk

GENERAL INFORMATION

Nearest Mainline Station: Sittingbourne (5 miles)
Nearest Bus Station: Sittingbourne
Car Parking: 500 spaces available – free parking
Coach Parking: Free parking available by appointment
Souvenir Shop(s): Yes
Food & Drinks: Yes

SPECIAL INFORMATION

A small but beautiful railway in rural Kent. The railway also has other attractions including a Model Railway, Traction Engines, a working Beam Engine, Vintage cars and tractors, a Locomotive Shed, a picnic site and woodland walks.

OPERATING INFORMATION

Opening Times: 2014 dates: Open on Easter Sunday then the first Sunday of the month from May to October and on Sunday 26th October. Open from 10.30am to 5.00pm
Steam Working: 11.00am to 4.30pm
Prices: Adult £10.00   Child £4.00

Detailed Directions by Car:
Take the M20 and exit at Junction 8 (Leeds Castle exit). Travel 4½ miles due north through Hollingbourne. The Railway is situated a little over 1 mile south of Bredgar village.

BURE VALLEY RAILWAY

Address: Aylsham Station, Norwich Road, Aylsham, Norfolk NR11 6BW
Telephone Nº: (01263) 733858
Year Formed: 1989
Location of Line: Aylsham to Wroxham
Length of Line: 9 miles

Nº of Steam Locos: 5
Nº of Other Locos: 3
Approx Nº of Visitors P.A.: 120,000
Gauge: 15 inches
Web Site: www.bvrw.co.uk
e-mail: info@bvrw.co.uk

GENERAL INFORMATION

Nearest Mainline Station: Wroxham (adjacent)
Nearest Bus Station: Aylsham (bus passes station)
Car Parking: Free parking for passengers at Aylsham and Wroxham Stations
Coach Parking: As above
Souvenir Shop(s): Yes at both Stations
Food & Drinks: Yes (Café at Aylsham opens daily)

SPECIAL INFORMATION

Boat trains connect at Wroxham with a 1½ hour cruise on the Norfolk Broads. Steam Locomotive driving courses are available throughout the year except in July and August. Some carriages are able to carry wheelchairs.

OPERATING INFORMATION

Opening Times: Aylsham Station is open daily. Trains run on various dates in 2014 including weekends in March and November and daily from 5th April to 2nd November, plus some other dates. Trains run from 10.00am to 5.25pm during high season. Open for Santa Specials on weekends and other dates in December. Please contact the railway for further details.
Steam Working: Most trains are steam hauled
Prices: Adult Return £12.50 (Single £8.00)
Child Return £6.50 (Single £5.00)
Family Return £33.00 (2 adult + 2 child)
Party discounts are available for groups of 20 or more if booked in advance.

Detailed Directions by Car:
From Norwich: Aylsham Station is situated midway between Norwich and Cromer on the A140 – follow the signs for Aylsham Town Centre. Wroxham Station is adjacent to the Wroxham British Rail Station – take the A1151 from Norwich; From King's Lynn: Take the A148 and B1354 to reach Aylsham Station.
Satellite Navigation: Use NR11 6BW for Aylsham Station and NR12 8UU for Wroxham Station.

CLEETHORPES COAST LIGHT RAILWAY

Address: King's Road, Cleethorpes, North East Lincolnshire DN35 0AG	**Nº of Steam Locos**: 9
Telephone Nº: (01472) 604657	**Nº of Other Locos**: 4
Year Formed: 1948	**Nº of Members**: 200
Location of Line: Lakeside Park & Marine embankment along Cleethorpes seafront	**Annual Membership Fee**: Adult £11.00
	Approx Nº of Visitors P.A.: 120,000
	Gauge: 15 inches
Length of Line: Almost 2 miles	**Web**: www.cleethorpescoastlightrailway.co.uk

GENERAL INFO

Nearest Mainline Station:
Cleethorpes (1 mile)
Nearest Bus Stop:
Meridian Point (opposite)
Car Parking: Boating Lake car park – 500 spaces (fee charged)
Coach Parking: As above
Souvenir Shop(s): Yes
Food & Drinks: Brief Encounters Tearoom and The Signal Box Inn are both located at Lakeside Station.

E-mail: adam.cowood@gmail.com

OPERATING INFO

Opening Times: 2014 dates: Open on weekends, Bank Holidays and during School Holidays throughout the year. Open daily during June, July and August. Also open for Santa Specials during December. Trains run from 10.00am to 6.00pm in the Summer months and from 10.50am to 4.20pm in the Winter months. Closed in November and January. Please contact the railway for further information.
Steam Working:
Most services are steam hauled
Prices: Adult Return £4.00
Child Return £3.50
Family Return £12.00
(2 Adult + 2 Child)
Tickets for Dogs £2.50
Note: Lower prices apply for shorter journeys and Under-3s travel free

Detailed Directions by Car:
Take the M180 to the A180 and continue to its' end. Follow signs for Cleethorpes. The Railway is situated along Cleethorpes seafront 1 mile south of the Pier. Look for the brown Railway Engine tourist signs and the main station is adjacent to the Leisure Centre.

THE CORRIS RAILWAY

Address: Station Yard, Corris, Machynlleth, Mid Wales SY20 9SH	**Nº of Steam Locos**: 1
Telephone Nº: (01654) 761303	**Nº of Other Locos**: 5
Year Formed: 1966	**Nº of Members**: 500
Location of Line: Corris to Maespoeth, Mid Wales	**Annual Membership Fee**: £20.00 (adult)
Length of Line: ¾ mile	**Approx Nº of Visitors P.A.**: 7,000
	Gauge: 2 feet 3 inches
	Web site: www.corris.co.uk
	E-mail: enquiries@corris.co.uk

GENERAL INFORMATION

Nearest Mainline Station: Machynlleth (5 miles)
Nearest Bus Station: Machynlleth (5 miles)
Car Parking: Available on site and also at the Corris Craft Centre (500 yards)
Coach Parking: Corris Craft Centre (please pre-book if visiting)
Souvenir Shop(s): Yes
Food & Drinks: Yes

SPECIAL INFORMATION

The Corris Railway originally ran from 1859 to 1948. A second locomotive and three carriages are currently being built and work on an extension to the partly-rebuilt line is currently underway.

OPERATING INFORMATION

Opening Times: 2014 dates: Open during Easter Weekend then every Sunday until 26th October, some Saturdays in May, all Saturdays in July and August, Mondays and Tuesdays during August and on all Bank Holiday weekends and Santa Specials run on 13th & 14th December.
The first train leaves Corris Station at 11.00am, the last train leaves at 4.00pm.
Steam Working: Most trains are steam-hauled.
Prices: Adult Return £6.00
        Child Return £3.00
        Senior Citizen Return £5.50
        Family Return £15.00
                (2 adults + 2 children)

Detailed Directions by Car:
From All Parts: Corris is situated off the A487 trunk road, five miles north of Machynlleth and 11 miles south of Dolgellau. Turn off the trunk road at the Braichgoch Hotel and the Station Yard is the 2nd turn on the right as you enter the village, just past the Holy Trinity Church and the Braich Goch Bunkhouse and Inn.

DERBYSHIRE DALES NARROW GAUGE RAILWAY

Correspondence: 44 Midland Terrace, Westhouses, Alfreton   DE55 5AB
Contact Phone Nº: (01629) 580381
Year Formed: 1998
Location of Line: Rowsley South Station, Peak Rail (SATNAV use DE4 2LF)
Length of Line: 500 yards

Nº of Steam Locos: None
Nº of Other Locos: 8
Approx Nº of Visitors P.A.: Not known
Gauge: 2 feet
Web site: www.peakrail.co.uk

GENERAL INFORMATION

Nearest Mainline Station: Matlock (4 miles)
Nearest Bus Station: Matlock (4 miles)
Car Parking: 200 spaces at Rowsley South Station
Coach Parking: Free parking at Rowsley South
Souvenir Shop(s): Yes
Food & Drinks: Yes

SPECIAL INFORMATION

This narrow gauge line is operated at Peak Rail's Rowsley South Station. The line has now been extended to 500 yards. Holders of valid Peak Rail tickets can travel free for one return journey.

OPERATING INFORMATION

Opening Times: Sundays and Bank Holiday weekends from April to early October.
Also open on certain Wednesdays in July and August – please contact the railway for further information.
Steam Working: None at present.
Prices: Adult £1.00
      Children 50p

Detailed Directions by Car:
Follow the A6 Bakewell to Matlock road to Rowsley then follow the brown tourist signs for the Peak Rail Station.

DEVON RAILWAY CENTRE

Address: Bickleigh, Tiverton, Devon, EX16 8RG
Telephone Nº: (01884) 855671
Year Formed: 1997
Location of Line: Bickleigh, Devon
Length of Line: ½ mile (2 foot and 7¼ inch gauges); 200 yards (Standard gauge)

Nº of Steam Locos: 1
Nº of Other Locos: 14
Approx Nº of Visitors P.A.: Not recorded
Gauge: 2 feet, 7¼ inches and Standard
Web site: www.devonrailwaycentre.co.uk
E-mail: matthew@devonrailwaycentre.freeserve.co.uk

GENERAL INFORMATION

Nearest Mainline Station: Exeter
Nearest Bus Station: Tiverton (Route 55)
Car Parking: Available on site
Coach Parking: Available on site
Souvenir Shop(s): Yes
Food & Drinks: Yes

SPECIAL INFORMATION

Devon Railway Centre has passenger carrying lines and also features a large model railway exhibition with 15 working layouts. A delightful Edwardian model village built to a 1:12 scale has recently been extended with a model funfair added.

OPERATING INFORMATION

Opening Times: 2014 dates: Daily from 5th to 27th April, 21st May to 7th September and 25th October to 2nd November. Closed on Mondays in June. Open Wednesday to Sunday inclusive from 3rd to 18th May and 10th to 28th September and also during weekends in October. Santa Specials run on dates in December. Open from 10.30am until 5.00pm on all operating days.
Steam Working: Trains may be steam or diesel hauled so please phone for further details.
Prices: Adult £7.80   Child £6.40
         Senior Citizen £7.00   Family £27.00
Admission includes unlimited train rides and access to the model village, model railways and museum.

Detailed Directions by Car:
From All Parts: Devon Railway Centre is situated adjacent to the famous Bickleigh Bridge, just off the A396 Exeter to Tiverton road (3 miles from Tiverton and 8 miles from Exeter).

Eastleigh Lakeside Steam Railway

Address: Lakeside Country Park, Wide Lane, Eastleigh, Hants. SO50 5PE	**Nº of Steam Locos:** 21
Telephone Nº: (023) 8061-2020	**Nº of Other Locos:** 3
Year Formed: 1992	**Approx Nº of Visitors P.A.:** 50,000
Location: Opposite Southampton airport	**Gauge:** 10¼ inches and 7¼ inches
Length of Line: 1¼ miles	**Web site:** www.steamtrain.co.uk

GENERAL INFORMATION

Nearest Mainline Station: Southampton Airport (Parkway) (¼ mile)
Nearest Bus Station: Eastleigh (1½ miles)
Car Parking: Free parking available on site
Coach Parking: Free parking available on site
Souvenir Shop(s): Yes
Food & Drinks: Cafe on site is open all year round from 9.00am to 4.00pm.

SPECIAL INFORMATION

The railway also has a playground and picnic area overlooking the lakes.

OPERATING INFORMATION

Opening Times: Weekends throughout the year and daily from mid-July until mid-September plus all other school holidays. Open 10.00am to 4.30pm (until 4.00pm during the winter months). Santa Specials run on some dates in December.
Steam Working: As above
Prices: Adult Return £3.00 (First Class £3.50)
Child Return £2.50 (First Class £3.00)

Tickets are available offering 3 return journeys at reduced rates. Annual season tickets are available. Children under the age of 2 years ride free of charge. Driver training courses can be booked in advance.

Detailed Directions by Car:
From All Parts: Exit the M27 at Junction 5 and take the A335 to Eastleigh. The Railway is situated ¼ mile past Southampton Airport Station on the left hand side of the A335.

EAST SUFFOLK LIGHT RAILWAY

Address: East Anglia Transport Museum, Chapel Road, Carlton Colville, Lowestoft NR33 8BL
Telephone Nº: (01502) 518459
Year Formed: 1972
Location: 3 miles south of Lowestoft
Length of Line: 200 yards

Nº of Steam Locos: None
Nº of Other Locos: 4
Approx Nº of Visitors P.A.: 18,000
Gauge: 2 feet
Web site: www.eatm.org.uk

GENERAL INFORMATION

Nearest Mainline Station: Oulton Broad South (2 miles)
Nearest Bus Station: Lowestoft (3 miles)
Car Parking: Available on site
Coach Parking: Available
Souvenir Shop(s): Yes
Food & Drinks: Available

SPECIAL INFORMATION

The railway is located at the East Anglia Transport Museum which also offers visitors trolleybus and tram rides.

OPERATING INFORMATION

Opening Times: Sundays and Thursdays from April to September, also Saturdays from June to September, Tuesdays and Wednesdays from 15th July to 3rd September and some other dates. Open from 1.00pm to 5.00pm on most days but from 11.00am to 5.00pm on Sundays and Bank Holidays.
Steam Working: None
Prices: Adults £8.00 (Admission and all rides)
Children £6.00 (Admission and all rides)
Concessions £7.00 (Admission and rides)

Detailed Directions by Car:
From All Parts: The East Anglia Transport Museum is clearly signposted by brown tourist signs from the A12, A146, A1117 and A1145.

Evesham Vale Light Railway

Address: Evesham Country Park, Twyford, Evesham WR11 4TP **Telephone Nº:** (01386) 422282 **Year Formed:** 2002 **Location of Line:** 1 mile north of Evesham **Length of Line:** 1¼ miles	**Nº of Steam Locos:** 3 **Nº of Other Locos:** 2 **Approx Nº of Visitors P.A.:** 50,000 **Gauge:** 15 inches **Web site:** www.evlr.co.uk **E-mail:** enquiries@evlr.co.uk

GENERAL INFORMATION

Nearest Mainline Station: Evesham (1 mile)
Nearest Bus Station: Evesham (1½ miles)
Car Parking: Available in the Country Park
Coach Parking: Available in the Country Park
Souvenir Shop(s): Yes
Food & Drinks: Restaurant at the Garden Centre

SPECIAL INFORMATION

The railway is situated within the 130 acre Evesham Country Park which has apple orchards and picnic areas overlooking the picturesque Vale of Evesham.

OPERATING INFORMATION

Opening Times: Open at weekends throughout the year and daily during school holidays. Trains run from 10.30am to 5.00pm (until 4.00pm during the winter). Please phone for further details.
Steam Working: Daily when trains are running.
Prices: Adult Return £2.30
Child Return £1.70
Senior Citizen Return £2.00
Note: Special reduced party rates are available for groups of 20 or more when booked in advance.

Detailed Directions by Car:
From the North: Exit the M42 at Junction 3 and take the A435 towards Alcester then the A46 to Evesham; From the South: Exit the M5 at Junction 9 and take the A46 to Evesham; From the West: Exit the M5 at Junction 7 and take the A44 to Evesham; From the East: Take the A44 from Oxford to Evesham. Upon reaching Evesham, follow the Brown tourist signs for Evesham Country Park and the railway.

EXBURY GARDENS RAILWAY

Address: Exbury Gardens, Exbury, Near Southampton SO45 1AZ
Telephone Nº: (02380) 891203
Year Formed: 2001
Location of Line: Exbury
Length of Line: 1¼ miles

Nº of Steam Locos: 3
Nº of Other Locos: 1
Approx Nº of Visitors P.A.: 55,000
Gauge: 12¼ inches
Web site: www.exbury.co.uk

Photograph courtesy of Gavin Clinton

GENERAL INFORMATION

Nearest Mainline Station: Brockenhurst (8 miles)
Nearest Bus Station: Hill Top (2½ miles)
The New Forest Open Tour Bus visits the gardens 8 times a day between 29th June and 15th September.
Car Parking: Free parking available on site
Coach Parking: Free parking available on site
Souvenir Shop(s): Yes
Food & Drinks: Available

SPECIAL INFORMATION

The railway is located in the world famous Rothschild azalea and rhododendron gardens at Exbury in the New Forest. A walk-through exhibition in the Engine Shed recalls the building of the steam railway.

OPERATING INFORMATION

Opening Times: 2014 dates: Daily from the 15th March to 2nd November. The gardens are open from 10.00am to 5.00pm (or dusk if earlier) and car park gates close at 6.00pm.
Steam Working: Most running days from 11.00am (restricted operation in March and September).
Prices: Adult Return £4.00
          Child Return £4.00   (Under-3s free)
Note: The above prices do not include admission to the Gardens which is required to visit the railway. Please check the Exbury web site for further details of entrance fees for the Gardens.

Detailed Directions by Car:
From all directions: Exit the M27 at Junction 2 and take the A326 to Dibden. Follow the brown tourist signs for Exbury Gardens & Steam Railway.

Fairbourne Railway

Address: Beach Road, Fairbourne, Dolgellau, Gwynedd LL38 2EX	**Nº of Steam Locos**: 4
Telephone Nº: (01341) 250362	**Nº of Other Locos**: 2
Year Formed: 1916	**Nº of Members**: 278
Location of Line: On A493 between Tywyn & Dolgellau	**Annual Membership Fee**: £25.00
	Approx Nº of Visitors P.A.: 18,000
Length of Line: 2 miles	**Gauge**: 12¼ inches
	Web Site: www.fairbournerailway.com

GENERAL INFORMATION

Nearest Mainline Station: Fairbourne (adjacent)
Nearest Bus Station: Fairbourne (adjacent)
Car Parking: Available in Mainline station car park
Coach Parking: Pay & Display car park 300 yards
Souvenir Shop(s): Yes
Food & Drinks: Yes – licensed Cafes at Fairbourne and Barmouth Ferry Terminus

SPECIAL INFORMATION

There is a connecting ferry service (foot passengers only) from Barmouth to Barmouth Ferry Terminus.

E-mail: fairbourne.rail@btconnect.com

OPERATING INFORMATION

Opening Times: 2014 dates: Open daily from 5th April until 30th October (closed on Mondays and Fridays except for School Holidays). The Little to Large Gala with an intensive timetable is on 25th & 26th May which features the 15-inch gauge visiting engines. Santa Specials run on 20th and 21st December.

Steam Working: The majority of services are steam-hauled.

Prices: Adult Return £9.00
Unaccompanied Child Return £5.25
(accompanied Children are £1.00 each)
Senior Citizen Return £8.00

Detailed Directions by Car:
From A470: Follow signs for Dolgellau and turn left onto A493 towards Tywyn. The turn-off for Fairbourne is located 8 miles south-west of Dolgellau; From South Wales: Follow signs for Machynlleth, then follow A487 towards Dolgellau. Then take A493 towards Fairbourne.

FAVERSHAM MINIATURE RAILWAY

Address: Brogdale Farm, Brogdale Road, Faversham, Kent ME13 8XZ
Telephone No: (01795) 474211
Year Formed: 1984
Location of Line: Faversham, Kent
Length of Line: 1 mile
Gauge: 9 inches

No of Steam Locos: 3
No of Other Locos: 9
No of Members: 40
Annual Membership Fee: £10.00 Adult, £40.00 Family
Approx No of Visitors P.A.: 6,000+
Web: www.favershamminiaturerailway.co.uk

GENERAL INFORMATION

Nearest Mainline Station: Faversham (¾ mile)
Nearest Bus Station: None, but a regular bus service travels to Faversham from Canterbury
Car Parking: Available on site
Coach Parking: Available on site
Souvenir Shop(s): Various shops on site
Food & Drinks: Available

SPECIAL INFORMATION

Faversham Miniature Railway is the only 9 inch gauge railway in the UK which is open to the public.

OPERATING INFORMATION

Opening Times: Sundays and Bank Holiday weekends from early March to November from 11.00am to 4.00pm. Also open for Santa Specials and other Special Events during the year. Please contact the railway for further information.
Steam Working: Special steam days only. Please contact the Railway for further details.
Prices: £1.50 per ride
  £2.00 per ride when Steam-hauled

Detailed Directions by Car:
Exit the M2 at Junction 5 and take the A251 towards Faversham. After about ½ mile turn left onto the A2 then left again after ¼ mile turning into Brogdale Road for the Farm and Railway.

FERRY MEADOWS MINIATURE RAILWAY

Address: Ham Lane, Nene Park,
Oundle Road, Peterborough   PE2 5UU
Telephone Nº: (01933) 398889
Year Formed: 1978
Location: Ferry Meadows, Nene Park
Length of Line: ½ mile

Nº of Steam Locos: 1
Nº of Other Locos: 2
Approx Nº of Visitors P.A.: 40,000
Gauge: 10¼ inches
Web site: www.ferrymeadowsrailway.co.uk

GENERAL INFORMATION

Nearest Mainline Station: Peterborough (2 miles)
Nearest Bus Station: Peterborough (2 miles)
Car Parking: Available adjacent
Coach Parking: Available adjacent
Souvenir Shop(s): Yes
Food & Drinks: Available

SPECIAL INFORMATION

The railway is situated in the Ferry Meadows area of
Nene Park in which watersports and other leisure
activities are also available.

OPERATING INFORMATION

Opening Times: 2014 dates: Every weekend from
1st March to 7th November and daily during the
school holidays.
Trains run from 11.30am to 4.30pm.
Steam Working: Every Sunday and some weekdays
during the School Holidays. Please contact the
railway for further details.
Prices: Adult Return £2.50   Adult Single £1.50
Child Return £2.00   Child Single £1.50

Detailed Directions by Car:
Nene Park is situated on the A605 Oundle Road. Follow the brown tourist signs for Nene Park.

FFESTINIOG RAILWAY

Address: Ffestiniog Railway, Harbour Station, Porthmadog, Gwynedd LL49 9NF
Telephone Nº: (01766) 516000
Year Formed: 1832
Location of Line: Porthmadog to Blaenau Ffestiniog
Length of Line: 13½ miles

Nº of Steam Locos: 12
Nº of Other Locos: 12
Nº of Members: 5,000
Annual Membership Fee: £26.00
Approx Nº of Visitors P.A.: 360,000
Gauge: 1 foot 11½ inches
Web Site: www.festrail.co.uk

GENERAL INFORMATION

Nearest Mainline Station: Blaenau Ffestiniog (interchange) or Minffordd
Nearest Bus Station: Bus stop next to stations at Porthmadog & Blaenau Ffestiniog
Car Parking: Parking available at Porthmadog, Blaenau Ffestiniog, Minffordd and Tan-y-Bwlch
Coach Parking: Available at Porthmadog and Blaenau Ffestiniog
Souvenir Shop(s): Yes
Food & Drinks: Yes

SPECIAL INFORMATION

The Railway runs through the spectacular scenery of Snowdonia National Park and the line now links up with the Welsh Highland Railway.

OPERATING INFORMATION

Opening Times: 2014 dates: Daily service from 25th March to 2nd November. A limited service operates in the Winter and Santa Specials run on December dates. Please contact the railway for further details.
Steam Working: Most trains are steam hauled.
Prices: Adult £21.00 (All-day Rover ticket)
Concessions £18.90 (All-day Rover ticket)
One child travels free with each adult, additional children travel for half the fare. Reductions are available groups of 20 or more. Cheaper fares are also available for single rides and shorter journeys.
E-mail: enquiries@festrail.co.uk

Detailed Directions by Car:
Portmadog is easily accessible from the Midlands – take the M54/A5 to Corwen then the A494 to Bala onto the A4212 to Trawsfynydd and the A470 (becomes the A487 from Maentwrog) to Porthmadog. From Chester take the A55 to Llandudno Junction and the A470 to Blaenau Ffestiniog. Both Stations are well-signposted.

GARTELL LIGHT RAILWAY

Address: Common Lane, Yenston, Templecombe, Somerset BA8 0NB	**Nº of Steam Locos**: 2
Telephone Nº: (01963) 370752	**Nº of Other Locos**: 3
Year Formed: 1991	**Approx Nº of Visitors P.A.**: 3,000
Location of Line: South of Templecombe	**Gauge**: 2 feet
Length of Line: ¾ mile	**Web site**: www.glr-online.co.uk

GENERAL INFORMATION

Nearest Mainline Station: Templecombe (1¼ miles)
Nearest Bus Station: Wincanton
Car Parking: Free parking adjacent to the station
Coach Parking: Adjacent to the station
Souvenir Shop(s): Yes
Food & Drinks: Meals, snacks and drinks available

SPECIAL INFORMATION

Part of the line runs along the track bed of the old Somerset & Dorset Joint Railway. The line has recently been extended and now features a working junction, flyover, road crossing and a new northern terminus

OPERATING INFORMATION

Opening Times: 2014 dates: 21st April; 5th May; 26th May; 29th June; 26th & 27th July (Steam & Vintage show); 24th & 25th August; 28th September and 26th October.
Trains depart at frequent intervals between 10.30am and 4.30pm.
Steam Working: Every day the railway operates.
Prices: Adult £7.50
Senior Citizen £6.00
Child £4.00
Family £20.00 (2 adults + 3 children)
Note: Tickets permit unlimited travel by any train on the day of purchase. Under-5s travel for free.

Detailed Directions by Car:
From All Parts: The Railway is situated off the A357 just south of Templecombe and on open days is clearly indicated by the usual brown tourist signs.

GIANT'S CAUSEWAY & BUSHMILLS RAILWAY

Address: Giant's Causeway Station, Runkerry Road, Bushmills, Co. Antrim, Northern Ireland   BT57 8SZ
Telephone Nº: (028) 2073-2844
Year Formed: 2002
Location: Between the distillery village of Bushmills and the Giant's Causeway
Length of Line: 2 miles

Nº of Steam Locos: 2
Nº of Other Locos: 2
Nº of Members: None
Approx Nº of Visitors P.A.: 50,000
Gauge: 3 feet
Web site: www.freewebs.com/giantscausewayrailway

GENERAL INFORMATION

Nearest Northern Ireland Railway Station: Coleraine/Portrush
Nearest Bus Station: Coleraine/Portrush
Car Parking: Car Park fee at Giant's Causeway Station is refunded upon ticket purchase. By parking at the Bushmills Station and taking the railway expensive parking charges at the Causeway itself can be avoided.
Coach Parking: Available on site
Souvenir Shop(s): Yes
Food & Drinks: At Giant's Causeway Station only

SPECIAL INFORMATION

The railway links the distillery village of Bushmills (open to visitors) to the World Heritage Site of the Giant's Causeway. The railway itself is built on the final two miles of the pioneering hydro-electric tramway which linked the Giant's Causeway to the main railway at Portrush from 1883 to 1949.

OPERATING INFORMATION

Opening Times: Daily in July and August, over St. Patrick's Day weekend and for Easter week. Also open at weekends from Easter to the end of June and in October & September. Trains run from 11.00am.
Steam Working: Please contact the railway for further information.
Prices: Adult Return £5.00
         Child Return £2.50
Note: Group rates are also available.

Detailed Directions by Car:
From Belfast take the M2 to the junction with the A26 (for Antrim, Ballymena and Coleraine). Follow the A26/M2/A26. From Ballymoney onwards Bushmills and the Giant's Causeway are well signposted. The railway is also well signposted in the immediate vicinity.

GOLDEN VALLEY LIGHT RAILWAY

Address: Butterley Station, Ripley,
Derbyshire   DE5 3QZ
Telephone Nº: (01773) 747674
Year Formed: 1987
Location of Line: Butterley, near Ripley
Length of Line: Four-fifths of a mile

Nº of Steam Locos: 2
Nº of Other Locos: 17
Nº of Members: 75
Annual Membership Fee: £16.00
Approx Nº of Visitors P.A.: 10,000
Gauge: 2 feet
Web site: www.gvlr.org.uk

GENERAL INFORMATION
Nearest Mainline Station: Alfreton (6 miles)
Nearest Bus Station: Bus stop outside the Station
Car Parking: Free parking at site – ample space
Coach Parking: Free parking at site
Souvenir Shop(s): Yes – at Butterley and Swanwick
Food & Drinks: Yes – both sites

SPECIAL INFORMATION
The Golden Valley Light Railway is part of the
Midland Railway – Butterley and runs from the
museum site through the country park to Newlands
Inn Station close to the Cromford Canal and the
pub of the same name.

OPERATING INFORMATION
Opening Times: 2014 dates: Weekends and Bank
Holidays from 5th April to 26th October and
Wednesdays to Sundays during the School Holidays.
Trains run from 11.50am to 3.55pm.
Steam Working: One weekend per month – please
contact the railway for further details.
Prices: Adult £2.00
          Children £1.00

Detailed Directions by Car:
From All Parts: From the M1 exit at Junction 28 and take the A38 towards Derby. The Centre is signposted at the
junction with the B6179.

GREAT LAXEY MINE RAILWAY

Address: Laxey Valley Gardens, Laxey, Isle of Man
Telephone Nº: (01624) 861706 (Secretary)
Year Formed: 2004
Location of Line: Laxey Valley Gardens
Length of Line: 550 yards

Nº of Steam Locos: 2
Nº of Other Locos: 1
Nº of Members: Approximately 300
Annual Membership Fee: £10.00
Approx Nº of Visitors P.A.: 7,000
Gauge: 19 inches
Web site: www.laxeyminerailway.im

GENERAL INFORMATION

Nearest Mainline Station: Laxey, Manx Electric Railway
Nearest Bus Station: Laxey
Car Parking: Available nearby
Coach Parking: Available nearby
Souvenir Shop(s): Yes
Food & Drinks: There are a number of Cafes nearby

SPECIAL INFORMATION

The Great Laxey Mine Railway is the recently restored surface section of the former mine tramway, the first section of which was opened in 1823. Originally worked by ponies, these were replaced by two steam locomotives in 1877. These engines were scrapped in 1935 but the restored line now uses two working replicas. A few minutes walk from the terminus of the railway is the Lady Isabella water wheel, the largest in the world. The railway itself is operated entirely by volunteers.

OPERATING INFORMATION

Opening Times: 2014 dates: Every Saturday and Bank Holiday from Easter until the end of September and also during every Sunday in August. A number of Special Event Days are operated throughout the season, details of which are advertised on the railway's web site.
Trains run from 11.00am to 4.30pm.
Steam Working: All trains are steam-hauled
Prices: Adult Return £2.00
Child Return £1.00 (Under-5s ride free)

Detailed Directions by Car:
Laxey is situated approximately 8 miles to the north east of Douglas on the A2 coast road.

GREAT WHIPSNADE RAILWAY

Address: ZSL Whipsnade Zoo, Dunstable LU6 2LF	**Nº of Steam Locos:** 2
Telephone Nº: (01582) 872171	**Nº of Other Locos:** 5
Year Formed: 1970	**Nº of Members:** None
Location of Line: ZSL Whipsnade Zoo, Near Dunstable	**Approx Nº of Visitors P.A.:** 130,000
	Gauge: 2 feet 6 inches
Length of Line: 1¾ miles	**Web site:** www.zsl.org

GENERAL INFORMATION

Nearest Mainline Station: Luton (7 miles)
Nearest Bus Station: Dunstable (3 miles)
Car Parking: Available just outside the park
Coach Parking: Available just outside the park
Souvenir Shop(s): Next to the Station
Food & Drinks: Available

SPECIAL INFORMATION

The Railway is situated in the ZSL Whipsnade Zoo operated by the Zoological Society of London.

OPERATING INFORMATION

Opening Times: The zoo is open daily from 10.00am throughout the year. Closing time varies from 4.00pm to 6.00pm depending on the time of the year. The railway runs daily from the Easter Holidays until the end of October half-term and at weekends at some other times of the year. Contact the zoo for further details.
Steam Working: Every operating day.
Prices: Adult £23.50   Child £17.00
                    Senior Citizen £21.28
Note: The above prices are for entrance into the Zoo itself and include a voluntary donation. Train rides are an additional charge:
Adults £4.50 Children £1.50 Concessions £4.00

Detailed Directions by Car:
From All Parts: Exit the M1 at Junction 11 and take the A505 then the B489. Follow signs for Whipsnade Zoo.

GROUDLE GLEN RAILWAY

Address: Groudle Glen, Onchan, Isle of Man
Telephone Nº: (01624) 670453 (weekends)
Year Formed: 1982   **Re-Opened:** 1986
Location of Line: Groudle Glen
Length of Line: ¾ mile
Gauge: 2 feet

Nº of Steam Locos: 2
Nº of Other Locos: 3
Nº of Members: 600
Annual Membership Fee: £15.00
Approx Nº of Visitors P.A.: 10,000
Correspondence: 29 Hawarden Avenue, Douglas, Isle of Man   IM1 4BP
Web site: www.ggr.org.uk

GENERAL INFORMATION

Nearest Mainline Station: Manx Electric Railway
Nearest Bus Station: Douglas Bus Station
Car Parking: At the entrance to the Glen
Coach Parking: At the entrance to the Glen
Souvenir Shop(s): Yes
Food & Drinks: Coffee and Tea available

SPECIAL INFORMATION

The Railway runs through a picturesque glen to a coastal headland where there are the remains of a Victorian Zoo. The Railway was built in 1896 and closed in 1962.

OPERATING INFORMATION

Opening Times: 2014 dates: Easter Sunday and Monday then Sundays from 4th May to 28th September 11.00am to 4.30pm. Also most Wednesday evenings from 18th June to 27th August – 7.00pm to 9.00pm.
Steam Working: Contact the Railway for details.
Prices: Adult Return £4.00
Child Return £2.00
Note: Joint fares are also available to include a Manx Electric Railway journey from Derby Castle.

Detailed Directions by Car:
The Railway is situated on the coast road to the north of Douglas.

HALL LEYS MINIATURE RAILWAY

Address: Hall Leys Park, Matlock, Derbyshire	**Nº of Steam Locos**: None
Telephone Nº: 07525 217116	**Nº of Other Locos**: 1
Year Formed: 1948	**Approx Nº of Visitors P.A.**: Not known
Location of Line: Hall Leys Park	**Gauge**: 9½ inches
Length of Line: 200 yards	

GENERAL INFORMATION

Nearest Mainline Station: Matlock (½ mile)
Nearest Bus Station: Matlock (by the train station)
Car Parking: Available near the train station on the new bypass
Coach Parking: As above

SPECIAL INFORMATION

The Hall Leys Miniature Railway has operated in Matlock since 1948 and is one of only 4 railways in the country to run a line with the unusual 9½ inch gauge. The park hosts a number of other attractions including a children's playground with a paddling pool, a lake with motor boats, a skate park and bowling and putting greens.

OPERATING INFORMATION

Opening Times: Weekends from mid-March to the end of September and daily during the school holidays in this period.
Steam Working: None at present.
Prices: 70p per ride.

Detailed Directions by Car:
Hall Leys Park is situated in the centre of Matlock between the River Derwent and the A615 Causeway Lane.

HASTINGS MINIATURE RAILWAY

Address: Rock-a-Nore Station, Old Town, Hastings TN34 3DW	**N° of Steam Locos**: None
Telephone N°: 07773 645228	**N° of Other Locos**: 7
Year Formed: 1948	**Approx N° of Visitors P.A.**: 20,000
Location: Between Hastings Old Town	**Gauge**: 10¼ inches
and the Historic Fishing Beach & Museum	**Web**: www.hastingsminiaturerailway.co.uk
Length of Line: 680 yards	

GENERAL INFORMATION

Nearest Mainline Station: Hastings (1 mile)
Car Parking: Limited parking available nearby
Coach Parking: None
Souvenir Shop(s): Yes
Food & Drinks: Available nearby

SPECIAL INFORMATION

The Hastings Miniature Railway, which opened on 5th June 1948, runs along the sea front area of Hastings Old Town and is a popular attraction.

OPERATING INFORMATION

Opening Times: Weekends throughout the year from 11.00am to 5.00pm (12.00pm to 4.00pm during the winter months) and also daily during through the School Holidays and during the Autumn half-term holidays.

Steam Working: None
Prices: Adult Return £3.00
        Child Return £3.00
        Adult Day Rover £7.00
        Child Day Rover £5.50
        Family Day Rover £22.00
                  (2 Adults + 2 Children)

Detailed Directions by Car:
The Railway is located to the eastern (Fisherman's End) of Hastings Old Town, just off the A259 and next to the Hastings Fishing Museum.

HAYLING SEASIDE RAILWAY

Address: Beachlands, Sea Front Road, Hayling Island, Hampshire PO11 0AG
Telephone Nº: 07775 696912
Year Formed: 2001
Location: Beachlands to Eastoke Corner
Length of Line: 1 mile
Web site: www.haylingseasiderailway.com

Nº of Steam Locos: Visiting locos only
Nº of Other Locos: 4
Nº of Members: Approximately 100
Annual Membership Fee: £10.00
Approx Nº of Visitors P.A.: 25,000
Gauge: 2 feet
E-mail: contact@haylingseasiderailway.com

GENERAL INFORMATION

Nearest Mainline Station: Havant
Nearest Bus Station: Beachlands
Car Parking: Spaces are available at both Beachlands and Eastoke Corner.
Coach Parking: Beachlands and Eastoke Corner
Souvenir Shop(s): Yes
Food & Drinks: Available

SPECIAL INFORMATION

The Railway runs along Hayling Island beach front where there are fantastic views across the Solent to the Isle of Wight.

OPERATING INFORMATION

Opening Times: Every Saturday, Sunday and Wednesday throughout the year and daily during the School holidays. Various specials run at different times of the year – please check the web site or phone the Railway for further details. The first train normally departs at 11.00am from Beachlands (from 10.00am on Wednesdays).
Steam Working: Visiting locos only. Please contact the railway for further information.
Prices: Adult Return £3.50
  Child/Senior Citizen Return £2.00
  Family Return £7.00 (2 Adult + 2 Child)
  Dogs travel free of charge!

Detailed Directions by Car:
Exit the A27 at Havant Roundabout and proceed to Hayling Island and Beachlands Station following the road signs. Parking is available south of the Carousel Amusement Park. Beachlands Station is within the car park.

HEATHERSLAW LIGHT RAILWAY

Address: Ford Forge, Heatherslaw,
Cornhill-on-Tweed TD12 4TJ
Telephone Nº: (01890) 820244
Year Formed: 1989
Location of Line: Ford & Etal Estates
between Wooler & Berwick
Length of Line: Almost 2½ miles

Nº of Steam Locos: 2
Nº of Other Locos: 1
Approx Nº of Visitors P.A.: 30,000
Gauge: 15 inches
Website: www.heatherslawlightrailway.co.uk
E-mail: info@heatherslawlightrailway.co.uk

GENERAL INFORMATION

Nearest Mainline Station: Berwick-upon-Tweed
(10 miles)
Nearest Bus Station: Berwick-upon-Tweed (10 mls)
Car Parking: Available on site
Coach Parking: Available on site
Souvenir Shop(s): Yes
Food & Drinks: Available

SPECIAL INFORMATION

The railway runs from Heatherslaw to Etel Castle
along the banks of the River Till. A choice of semi-
open and fully enclosed coaches are available to
passengers, even on the wettest of days!

OPERATING INFORMATION

Opening Times: 2014 dates: Daily from 30th
March to 2nd November. Trains run hourly from
11.00am to 3.00pm (until 4.00pm in July & August)
Steam Working: Daily except when maintenance is
is being carried out on the engine.
Prices: Adult Return £6.50
Child Return £4.50   (Under 5's: £2.50)
Senior Citizen Return £6.00

Detailed Directions by Car:
From the North: Take the A697 from Coldstream and the railway is about 5 miles along.
From the South: Take the A697 from Wooler and Millfield.

ISLE OF MAN STEAM RAILWAY

Address: Isle of Man Railways, Banks Circus, Douglas, Isle of Man   IM1 5PT
Telephone Nº: (01624) 662525
Year Formed: 1873
Location of Line: Douglas to Port Erin
Length of Line: 15½ miles

Nº of Steam Locos: 7
Nº of Other Locos: 2
Approx Nº of Visitors P.A.: 140,000
Gauge: 3 feet
Web site: www.iombusandrail.info

GENERAL INFORMATION

Nearest Mainline Station: Not applicable
Car Parking: Limited parking at all stations
Coach Parking: Available at Port Erin
Souvenir Shop(s): Souvenirs are available from all manned stations and from the shop at Port Erin Railway Museum
Food & Drinks: Yes – Douglas & Port Erin stations

SPECIAL INFORMATION

The Isle of Man Steam Railway is operated by the Isle of Man Government. A number of special events are held at the railway throughout the year.

OPERATING INFORMATION

Opening Times: 2014 Dates: Weekends and School Holidays from 7th March to late May then daily until 5th November. Day and evening services are available during the summer months. Please contact the railway or check the web site for further details.
Steam Working: All scheduled services
Prices: Prices vary with 1, 3, 5 & 7 day Explorer tickets also available which include travel on buses, the Snaefell and Manx Electric Railways and Douglas Corporation Horse Trams. Railcards and Season Tickets are also available.

Detailed Directions:
By Sea from Heysham (Lancashire) or Liverpool to reach Isle of Man. By Air from Belfast, Birmingham, Blackpool, Dublin, Glasgow, Gloucester, Jersey, Liverpool, Manchester, Newcastle, Bristol and London. Douglas Station is ½ mile inland from the Sea Terminal at the end of North Quay.

KERR'S MINIATURE RAILWAY

Address: West Links Park, Arbroath, Tayside, Scotland	**Nº of Steam Locos:** 2
Telephone Nº: (01241) 874074 or 879249	**Nº of Other Locos:** 4
Year Formed: 1935	**Approx Nº of Visitors P.A.:** 10,000
Location: Seafront, West Links Park	**Gauge:** 10¼ inches
Length of Line: 400 yards	**Website:** www.kerrsminiaturerailway.co.uk
	E-mail: info@kerrsminiaturerailway.co.uk

GENERAL INFORMATION

Nearest Mainline Station: Arbroath (1½ miles)
Nearest Bus Station: Arbroath (1½ miles)
Car Parking: Available 600 yards from railway
Coach Parking: Available 600 yards from railway
Souvenir Shop(s): Gifts available
Food & Drinks: Cafe stall in West Links Park

SPECIAL INFORMATION

The Railway is Scotland's oldest passenger-carrying miniature railway. It is a family-run enterprise not run for profit which is staffed by volunteers. The track itself runs alongside the Dundee to Aberdeen mainline.

OPERATING INFORMATION

Opening Times: 2014 dates: Daily during the Easter Holidays (5th April to 21st April) then weekends from 29th March to the end of September. Open daily from 28th June to 31st August. Opening times are 11.00am to 4.00pm.
Steam Working: No set pattern but Steam is more likely to be running on Sundays than other dates.
Prices: Adults £1.50
Children £1.00

Detailed Directions by Car:

From All Parts: West Links Park is a seaside location which runs parallel to the A92 Coastal Tourist Route in Arbroath. Turn off the A92 at the West Links Park/KMR sign. The railway is then 600 yards due West along the seafront.

KIRKLEES LIGHT RAILWAY

Address: Park Mill Way, Clayton West, near Huddersfield, W. Yorks. HD8 9XJ	**Nº of Steam Locos:** 4
Telephone Nº: (01484) 865727	**Nº of Other Locos:** 2
Year Formed: 1991	**Approx Nº of Visitors P.A.:** 48,000
Location of Line: Clayton West to Shelley	**Gauge:** 15 inches
Length of Line: 4 miles	**Web site:** www.kirkleeslightrailway.com

Photograph courtesy of Karen Ashton

GENERAL INFORMATION

Nearest Mainline Station: Denby Dale (4 miles)
Nearest Bus Station: Bus stops at the bottom of Park Mill Way. Take the 435 and 436 from Wakefield or the 80 and 81 from Huddersfield.
Car Parking: Ample free parking at site
Coach Parking: Ample free parking at site
Souvenir Shop(s): Yes
Food & Drinks: Yes

SPECIAL INFORMATION

The Railway now has outdoor play areas for children, a 7¼ inch railway at Clayton West and Shelley Tearooms open during railway operations.

OPERATING INFORMATION

Opening Times: 2014 dates: Every weekend and Bank Holiday throughout the year and daily during school holidays. Open Wednesday to Sunday from 4th June to 20th July and daily from 16th July to 3rd September.
Steam Working: All trains are steam-hauled (subject to availability). Train timetables vary, so please check the website for further information.
Prices: Adults £7.00
 Children (3-16 years) £5.00
 Children (under 3 years) Free of charge
 Concessions £6.00
 Family Ticket £22.00
Note: Prices at Special events may vary.

Detailed Directions by Car:
The Railway is located on the A636 Wakefield to Denby Dale road. Turn off the M1 at Junction 39 and follow the A636 signposted for Denby Dale. Continue for approximately 4 miles then the railway is on the left after passing under the railway bridge and is situated at the top of the Industrial Estate, just before the village of Scissett.

LAKESHORE RAILROAD

Address: South Marine Park, South Shields NE33 2LD	**N° of Steam Locos:** 2
Telephone N°: (0191) 454-7761	**N° of Other Locos:** 1
Year Formed: 1972	**Approx N° of Visitors P.A.:** 65,000
Length of Line: 570 yards	**Gauge:** 9½ inches
	Web site: None

GENERAL INFORMATION

Nearest Mainline Station: South Shields (¾ mile)
Nearest Bus Station: Newcastle (11 miles)
Car Parking: Available on the seafront
Coach Parking: Available nearby
Souvenir Shop(s): None
Food & Drinks: Available nearby

SPECIAL INFORMATION

The Lakeshore Railroad runs two American-designed locomotives – hence the name!

OPERATING INFORMATION

Opening Times: Weekends throughout the year and daily from mid-May to mid-September and during other School Holidays except for Christmas. Trains run from 11.00am to 5.00pm.
Steam Working: Daily, subject to availability
Prices: Adults £1.20
Children £1.20 (Free for Under-3s)

Detailed Directions by Car:
From All Parts: Take the A194 into South Shields. The railway is located by the Seafront in South Marine Park and can be found by following the brown tourist signs marked for the 'Seafront'.

LAPPA VALLEY STEAM RAILWAY

Address: St. Newlyn East, Newquay, Cornwall   TR8 5LX
Telephone Nº: (01872) 510317
Year Formed: 1974
Location of Line: Benny Halt to East Wheal Rose, near St. Newlyn East
Length of Line: 1 mile

Nº of Steam Locos: 2
Nº of Other Locos: 2
Approx Nº of Visitors P.A.: 50,000
Gauge: 15 inches
Web site: www.lappavalley.co.uk

GENERAL INFORMATION

Nearest Mainline Station: Newquay (5 miles)
Nearest Bus Station: Newquay (5 miles)
Car Parking: Free parking at Benny Halt
Coach Parking: Free parking is available at Benny Halt
Souvenir Shop(s): Yes
Food & Drinks: Yes

SPECIAL INFORMATION

The railway runs on part of the former Newquay to Chacewater branch line. Site also has a Grade II listed mine building, boating, play areas for children and 2 other miniature train rides.

OPERATING INFORMATION

Opening Times: 2014 dates: Daily from 3rd April to 31st August. Then daily from 1st to 28th September (but closed on Saturdays). Open from Sunday to Thursday only from 29th September to 24th October then daily from 25th to 31st October.
Steam Working: 10.30am to 4.30pm during the summer months.
Prices: Adult £12.00 (Off-peak £9.00)
        Child £9.50 (Off-peak £6.70)
        Family £37.00 (Off-peak £30.00)
            (2 adults + 2 children)
        Family £40.00 (Off-peak £32.00)
            (2 adults + 3 children)
        Senior Citizen £10.00
            (Off-peak £7.00)

Detailed Directions by Car:
The railway is signposted from the A30 at the Summercourt-Mitchell bypass, from the A3075 south of Newquay and the A3058 east of Newquay.

LAUNCESTON STEAM RAILWAY

Address: The Old Gasworks, St. Thomas Road, Launceston, Cornwall PL15 8DA
Telephone Nº: (01566) 775665
Year Formed: Opened in 1983
Location of Line: Launceston to Newmills
Length of Line: 2½ miles

Nº of Steam Locos: 4
Nº of Other Locos: 4
Gauge: 1 foot 11 ⅝ inches
Web site: www.launcestonsr.co.uk

GENERAL INFORMATION

Nearest Mainline Station: Liskeard (15 miles)
Nearest Bus Station: Launceston (½ mile)
Car Parking: At Station, Newport Industrial Estate, Launceston
Coach Parking: As above
Souvenir Shop(s): Yes – also with a bookshop
Food & Drinks: Cafe serving hot and cold meals

SPECIAL INFORMATION

The Launceston Steam Railway runs for two and a half miles through the glorious Kensey Valley along the trackbed of the old North Cornwall Railway, where once express trains from Waterloo passed.

OPERATING INFORMATION

Opening Times: 2014 dates: 13th to 25th April; 18th to 30th May (closed on 24th May). Sundays, Mondays and Tuesdays in June. Daily from 1st July until the 26th September but closed on Saturdays. Also open daily from 26th to 31st October.
Steam Working: Hourly from 11.00am to 4.00pm.
Prices: Adult £9.50
Child £6.20
Family £27.00 (2 adults + 4 children)
Senior Citizen £8.20
Group rates are available upon application.

Detailed Directions by Car:
From the East/West: Drive to Launceston via the A30 and look for the brown Steam Engine Tourist signs. Use the L.S.R. car park at the Newport Industrial Estate; From Bude/Holsworthy: Take the A388 to Launceston and follow signs for the town centre. After the river bridge turn left at the traffic lights into Newport Industrial Estate and use the L.S.R. car park. Sat Navs use the following post code: PL15 8EX.

LEADHILLS & WANLOCKHEAD RAILWAY

Address: The Station, Leadhills,
Lanarkshire   ML12 6XP
Telephone Nº: None
Year Formed: 1983
Location of Line: Leadhills, Lanarkshire
Length of Line: ¾ mile (at present)

Nº of Steam Locos: 1 (Not in operation)
Nº of Other Locos: 5
Nº of Members: Approximately 100
Annual Membership Fee: Adult £15.00
Approx Nº of Visitors P.A.: 3,500
Gauge: 2 feet
Web site: www.leadhillsrailway.co.uk

GENERAL INFORMATION

Nearest Mainline Station: Sanquhar
Nearest Bus Station: Lanark and Sanquhar
Car Parking: Available on site
Coach Parking: Available on site
Souvenir Shop(s): Yes
Food & Drinks: Yes

SPECIAL INFORMATION

Leadhills & Wanlockhead Railway is the highest
adhesion railway in the UK with the summit 1,498
feet above sea level.

OPERATING INFORMATION

Opening Times: Weekends from Easter until the
end of September. Trains run from 11.20am to
4.20pm on operating days.
Steam Working: None at present
Prices: Adult Day Ticket £4.00
Child Day Ticket £2.00
Family Day Ticket £10.00
        (2 adults and up to 2 children)
Concession Day Ticket £3.00

Detailed Directions by Car:
From the South: Exit the M74 at Junction 14 and follow the A702 to Elvanfoot. Turn right onto the B7040 and
follow to Leadhills. Turn left at the T-junction and Station Road is a short distance on the left; From the North: Exit
the M74 at Junction 13 for Abington and follow signs for Leadhills along the B797. Station Road is on the left
shortly after entering Leadhills.

LEEDS INDUSTRIAL MUSEUM

Address: Canal Road, Armley, Leeds, LS12 2QF
Telephone Nº: (0113) 263-7861
Year Formed: 1985
Location of Line: Armley Mills, Leeds
Length of Line: ¼ mile

Nº of Steam Locos: 8 (One in steam)
Nº of Other Locos: 31 (One operational)
Approx Nº of Visitors P.A.: 42,000
Gauges: 2 feet and 18 inches
Web site: www.leeds.gov.uk/ArmleyMills

GENERAL INFORMATION

Nearest Mainline Station: Leeds City (2 miles)
Nearest Bus Station: Leeds (2 miles)
Car Parking: Available on site
Coach Parking: Available
Souvenir Shop(s): Yes
Food & Drinks: Tea and coffee only

SPECIAL INFORMATION

A number of Leeds-built locomotives are on display at the museum in addition to a variety of static engines and machinery.

OPERATING INFORMATION

Opening Times: Closed on Mondays but otherwise, daily throughout the year. Open on Bank Holiday Mondays, however. Open from 10.00am to 5.00pm (but from 1.00pm to 5.00pm on Sundays).
Steam Working: Bank Holidays and the last weekend in September.
Prices: Adults £3.30
     Children £1.20
     Concessions £1.70
     Family Ticket £6.50
Lower prices are charged to "Leeds Card" holders.
Note: The line is used for demonstrations only – unfortunately, rides are not available.

Detailed Directions by Car:
From All Parts: The Museum is located next to the Cardigan Field Leisure Complex which is just to the South of the A65 Kirkstall Road.

LEIGHTON BUZZARD RAILWAY

Address: Pages Park Station, Billington Road, Leighton Buzzard, Beds. LU7 4TN
Telephone Nº: (01525) 373888
E-mail: info@buzzrail.co.uk
Year Formed: 1967
Location of Line: Leighton Buzzard
Length of Line: 3 miles

Nº of Steam Locos: 8
Nº of Other Locos: 8
Nº of Members: 400
Annual Membership Fee: £21.00
Approx Nº of Visitors P.A.: 20,000
Gauge: 2 feet
Web site: www.buzzrail.co.uk

GENERAL INFORMATION

Nearest Mainline Station: Leighton Buzzard (2 miles)
Nearest Bus Station: Leighton Buzzard (¾ mile)
Car Parking: Free parking adjacent
Coach Parking: Free parking adjacent
Souvenir Shop(s): Yes   **Food & Drinks:** Yes

SPECIAL INFORMATION

The railway was constructed in 1919 to carry sand from local quarries using surplus materials from World War I battlefield supply lines. Now a working museum, it transports passengers and is operated by volunteers.

OPERATING INFORMATION

Opening Times: 2014 dates: Sundays from 16th March to 26th October plus Bank Holiday weekends. Also open on some Saturdays and weekdays. Trains run from 10.40am to 3.40pm and Santa Specials run on some dates in December. Please contact the railway or visit their web site for further details.
Steam Working: Most operating days.
Prices: Adult £9.50
Child £5.50
Senior Citizens £8.00
Note: A variety of Family Tickets, Day Rover tickets and Single tickets are also available.

Detailed Directions by Car:
Travel to Leighton Buzzard then follow the brown tourist signs showing a steam train. Pages Park Station is ¾ mile to the south of the Town Centre. From the A505/A4146 bypass, turn towards Leighton Buzzard at the roundabout following the 'Narrow Gauge Railway' brown tourist signs.

LINCOLNSHIRE COAST LIGHT RAILWAY

Address: Skegness Water Leisure Park, Walls Lane, Skegness PE25 1JF
Telephone Nº: (01754) 897400
E-mail: johnchappell@ricsonline.org
Year Formed: 1960 (re-opened in 2009)
Location of Line: Skegness
Length of Line: ¾ miles

Nº of Steam Locos: 1 awaiting restoration
Nº of Other Locos: 4
Nº of Members: Approximately 50
Approx Nº of Visitors P.A.: 5,000
Gauge: 2 feet
Web site: www.lincolnshire-coast-light-railway.co.uk

GENERAL INFORMATION

Nearest Mainline Station: Skegness (3 miles)
Nearest Bus Station: Skegness (3 miles)
Car Parking: Free parking available on site
Coach Parking: Free parking available on site
Souvenir Shop(s): None
Food & Drinks: Available

SPECIAL INFORMATION

The railway was originally located some distance up the coast at the Cleethorpes/Humberston 'Fitties' before closure during the 1980s.

OPERATING INFORMATION

Opening Times: 2014 dates: 24th & 25th May; 26th July; 2nd, 9th, 16th, 23rd and 24th August. A special Gala Day will be held on 14th June when our historic First World War trench railway vehicles will be demonstrated with guided tours of our collection available.
Steam Working: None at present.
Prices: Adults £1.00
          Children £1.00

Detailed Directions by Car:

From All Parts: Take the A52 North from Skegness (signposted for Ingoldmells) and continue for 3 miles. Turn left onto Walls Lane opposite the Butlins signposted for the Water Leisure Park. After ¼ mile turn left into the Park and follow the signs for the Railway.

LITTLEHAMPTON RAILWAY

Address: Mewsbrook Park,
Littlehampton   BN16 2LX
Telephone N°: (01460) 221303
Year Formed: 1948
Location of Line: Mewsbrook Park
Length of Line: ½ mile

N° of Steam Locos: 1 (visiting loco)
N° of Other Locos: 1
N° of Members: Approximately 50
Approx N° of Visitors P.A.: 18,000
Gauge: 12¼ inches
Website: www.littlehamptonrailway.co.uk
E-mail: info@littlehamptonrailway.co.uk

GENERAL INFORMATION

Nearest Mainline Station: Littlehampton (1 mile)
Nearest Bus Station: Littlehampton
Car Parking: Available at the swimming pool, at East Green and along the Sea Wall.
Coach Parking: Available at the swimming pool
Souvenir Shop(s): During special event days only
Food & Drinks: Cafes are adjacent to both stations

SPECIAL INFORMATION

The Littlehampton Railway is the oldest 12¼ inch gauge railway in the UK and runs from Mewsbrook Park to Norfolk Gardens. The railway is surrounded by a variety of leisure attractions including a boating lake and a 9-hole golf course.

OPERATING INFORMATION

Opening Times: Weekends and School Holidays from early February to the end of October (weather permitting). Trains run daily from 12.00am to 4.00pm and from 10.00am to 5.00pm in July and August.
Steam Working: The railway hopes to have a guest loco steaming for part of the year. Please contact the railway for further information.
Prices: Adult Return £3.00
Child Return £2.00
Family Ticket Return £9.00
Note: High fares apply for special event days.

Detailed Directions by Car:
From All Parts: Take the A27 Brighton to Portsmouth road and follow signs for Littlehampton. Upon entering Littlehampton, follow signs for the Swimming Pool/Sea Front and, when you reach the Beach Road (which runs along parallel to the sea), head east and park either at East Green or further along to the Swimming Pool.

LLANBERIS LAKE RAILWAY

Address: Gilfach Ddu, Llanberis, Gwynedd LL55 4TY
Telephone N°: (01286) 870549
Year Formed: 1970
Location of Line: Just off the A4086 Caernarfon to Capel Curig road at Llanberis
Length of Line: 2½ miles

N° of Steam Locos: 3
N° of Other Locos: 4
Approx N° of Visitors P.A.: 80,000
Gauge: 1 foot 11½ inches
Web site: www.lake-railway.co.uk

GENERAL INFORMATION

Nearest Mainline Station: Bangor (8 miles)
Nearest Bus Station: Caernarfon (6 miles) (there is a bus stop by Llanberis Station)
Car Parking: £4.00 Council car park on site
Coach Parking: Ample free parking on site
Souvenir Shop(s): Yes
Food & Drinks: Yes

SPECIAL INFORMATION

Llanberis Lake Railway runs along part of the trackbed of the Padarn Railway which transported slates for export and closed in 1961.

OPERATING INFORMATION

Opening Times: 2014 dates: Open most days from 23rd March to 1st November, daily from 18th May to 5th September and on certain days during the winter. Please send for a free timetable or check out the railway's web site where an online booking feature is now available.
Steam Working: Every operating day.
Trains generally run from 11.00am to 4.00pm.
Prices: Adult £7.80   Child £4.50
      Concessions £7.00
      Family ticket £20.00 (2 Adult + 2 Children)
A range of other family discounts are also available.
Note: The Welsh Slate Museum is situated adjacent to the Railway.

Detailed Directions by Car:
The railway is situated just off the A4086 Caernarfon to Capel Curig road. Follow signs for Padarn Country Park.

LYNTON & BARNSTAPLE RAILWAY

Address: Woody Bay Station, Martinhoe Cross, Parracombe, Devon EX31 4RA	**Nº of Steam Locos:** 2
	Nº of Other Locos: 3
Telephone Nº: (01598) 763487	**Nº of Members:** 2,200
E-mail: enquiries@lynton-rail.co.uk	**Annual Membership Fee:** £26.00
Year Formed: 1993	**Approx Nº of Visitors P.A.:** 35,000
Location of Line: North Devon	**Gauge:** 1 foot 11½ inches
Length of Line: One mile	**Web site:** www.lynton-rail.co.uk

Photo courtesy of Trevor A. Garnham

GENERAL INFORMATION

Nearest Mainline Station: Barnstaple
Nearest Bus Station: Barnstaple
Car Parking: Available at Woody Bay Station
Coach Parking: Available by prior arrangement
Souvenir Shop(s): Yes – at Woody Bay Station
Food & Drinks: Available at Woody Bay Station

SPECIAL INFORMATION

New for 2014: Original Lynton & Barnstaple Railway carriages built in 1898 and 1903 are now operating a regular passenger service.

OPERATING INFORMATION

Opening Times: Open most days from Easter until the end of October and selected dates in December. Please check with the railway for exact dates. Trains run from 10.45am to 4.00pm.
Steam Working: Most trains are steam-hauled except on Mondays and Fridays outside of the school holidays or in the event of breakdown.
Prices: Adult Return £7.50
Child Return £3.00 (Under-14s)
Senior Citizen Return £6.00
Family Ticket £18 (2 Adults + 3 Children)
Note: Upgrades to First Class are available for £3.00 per person.

Detailed Directions by Car:
From All Parts: Woody Bay Station is located alongside the A39 halfway between Lynton and Blackmoor Gate and one mile north-east of the village of Parracombe.

MARGAM PARK RAILWAY

Address: Margam Country Park, Port Talbot SA13 2TJ **Telephone Nº:** (01639) 881635 **Year Formed:** 1976 **Location of Line:** Margam Country Park **Length of Line:** Almost 1½ miles	**Nº of Steam Locos:** None **Nº of Other Locos:** 1 **Approx Nº of Visitors P.A.:** 200,000 (to the Park itself) **Gauge:** 2 feet **Web site:** www.margamcountrypark.co.uk

GENERAL INFORMATION

Nearest Mainline Station: Port Talbot (3 miles)
Nearest Bus Station: Port Talbot (3 miles)
Car Parking: Available on site for a £3.50 charge
Coach Parking: Available
Souvenir Shop(s): Yes
Food & Drinks: Available

SPECIAL INFORMATION

Set in 1,000 acres of glorious parkland, Margam Country Park features an 18th Century Orangery, a Tudor-Gothic Victorian Mansion House and a 12th Century Chapter House.

OPERATING INFORMATION

Opening Times: 2014 dates: Daily from 5th April to 31st August. Trains run from 10.00am to 4.15pm.
Steam Working: None at present
Prices: Adults £1.80
Children £1.00
Concessions £1.00
Family Ticket £4.60 (2 adults + 2 children)

Detailed Directions by Car:
From All Parts: Exit the M4 at Junction 38 and take the A48 towards Pyle following the brown tourist signs for Margam Country Park. The Park is situated on the left hand side of the road.

MOSELEY INDUSTRIAL NARROW GAUGE TRAMWAY, TOY AND MINING MUSEUM

Address: Tumblydown Farm, Tolgus Mount, Redruth   TR15 3TA
Telephone Nº: (01209) 211191
Alternative Telephone Nº: 07511 256677
Year Formed: 1969 (formed in the northwest, relocated to Cornwall in 2000)
Location: ½ mile north of Redruth

Length of Line: 600 yards
Nº of Steam Locos: 1 road locomotive
Nº of Other Locos: 16
Approx Nº of Visitors P.A.: 4,000
Gauge: 2 feet
Web site: www.moseleymuseum.co.uk

GENERAL INFORMATION

Nearest Mainline Station: Redruth (2 miles)
Nearest Bus Station: Redruth (2 miles)
Car Parking: Available on site
Coach Parking: Available by prior arrangement
Souvenir Shop(s): Yes
Food & Drinks: Available by prior arrangement

SPECIAL INFORMATION

Moseley Museum is operated by volunteers who maintain and restore the vehicles and displays. Other attractions at the museum include collections of vintage toys and meccano, curios and mining equipment. Home of the Murdoch Flyer.

OPERATING INFORMATION

Opening Times: Open throughout the year for group and individual visits by prior arrangement, plus a number of special public open days. Also open on some Monday and Thursday afternoons. Please contact the museum for further details before visiting.
Steam Working: Operational road locomotive, 'The Murdoch Flyer'.
Prices: Free of charge but voluntary donations are gratefully received!

Detailed Directions by Car:
From the A30, turn on to the old Redruth bypass (A3047). Follow the brown tourist signs for Trickys Hotel. Tumblydown Farm is on the right about 200 yards past Trickys Hotel.

NATIONAL COAL MINING MUSEUM FOR ENGLAND

Address: Caphouse Colliery, New Road, Overton, Wakefield WF4 4RH
Telephone Nº: (01924) 848806
Year Formed: 1988
Location of Line: West Yorkshire
Length of Line: 500 yards

Nº of Steam Locos: None in service
Nº of Other Locos: 2
Approx Nº of Visitors P.A.: 110,000 (to the Museum)
Gauge: 2 feet 6 inches
Web site: www.ncm.org.uk

GENERAL INFORMATION

Nearest Mainline Station: Wakefield (5 miles)
Nearest Bus Station: Wakefield (5 miles)
Car Parking: Available on site
Coach Parking: Available
Souvenir Shop(s): Yes
Food & Drinks: Available

SPECIAL INFORMATION

The National Coal Mining Museum for England offers an unusual combination of exciting experiences. The highlight of any visit is the underground tour where experienced local miners guide parties around the underground workings. Each visitor is provided with a hat, belt and battery, so that the true atmosphere of working life underground is captured. Above ground there are genuine pit ponies, a train ride, machinery displays, steam winder, pithead baths and the 42-acre rural site with its nature trail and adventure playground to be enjoyed. In addition, a modern visitor centre has been built with multimedia audio-visual displays, galleries and exhibitions, a licensed cafe and well-stocked shop.

OPERATING INFORMATION

Opening Times: Daily throughout the year except for Christmas Day, Boxing Day and New Year's Day. Open from 10.00am to 5.00pm.
Steam Working: None
Prices: Admission to the Museum is free of charge. Return train rides are £1.00 per person.

Detailed Directions by Car:
From All Parts: Take the M1 to Wakefield and follow the brown tourist signs for the National Coal Mining Museum which is at the side of the A642 in Overton.

Newby Hall Miniature Railway

Address: Newby Hall & Gardens, near Ripon HG4 5AE	**Nº of Steam Locos**: 1
Telephone Nº: 0845 450-4068	**Nº of Other Locos**: 2
Year Formed: 1971	**Nº of Members**: None
Location of Line: Newby Hall, Ripon	**Approx Nº of Passengers P.A.**: 60,000
Length of Line: Approximately 1 mile	**Gauge**: 10¼ inches
	Web site: www.newbyhall.com

GENERAL INFORMATION

Nearest Mainline Station: Knaresborough (7 miles)
Nearest Bus Station: Ripon (3 miles)
Car Parking: Free parking available on site
Coach Parking: Available
Souvenir Shop(s): No specific railway souvenirs
Food & Drinks: Available

SPECIAL INFORMATION

The railway is located within the gardens of Newby Hall and the track runs alongside the scenic River Ure.

OPERATING INFORMATION

Opening Times: 2014 dates: Open daily from 1st April until 28th September from 11.00am to 5.30pm. Trains operate at regular intervals throughout the day.
Steam Working: Please contact the railway for further information.
Prices: Return Ticket £1.60
Note: The price above is for train rides only. Entrance to the House and Gardens is an additional charge which must be paid to gain entry to the grounds.

Detailed Directions by Car:
From All Parts: Exit the A1(M) at Junction 48 and follow the signs for Newby Hall towards Ripon briefly along the A168. At the Langthorpe roundabout follow the brown tourist signs for Newby Hall (passing under the A1(M)) and the Hall is approximately 2 miles.

NORTH BAY MINIATURE RAILWAY

Address: Burniston Road, Scarborough, North Yorkshire YO12 6PF	**Nº of Steam Locos**: None
Telephone Nº: (01723) 368791	**Nº of Other Locos**: 4
Year Opened: 1931	**Nº of Members**: None
Location: Peasholm Park to Scalby Mills	**Approx Nº of Visitors P.A.**: 200,000
Length of Line: 1 mile	**Gauge**: 20 inches
	Web site: www.nbr.org.uk

GENERAL INFORMATION

Nearest Mainline Station: Scarborough
Nearest Bus Station: Scarborough
Car Parking: Adjacent to the railway
Coach Parking: Adjacent to the railway
Souvenir Shop(s): Yes
Food & Drinks: Glass House Cafe in Peasholm Park

SPECIAL INFORMATION

The North Bay Miniature Railway was opened in 1931 and operates between Northstead Manor and Scalby Mills for the Sea Life Centre.

OPERATING INFORMATION

Opening Times: 2014 dates: Daily from 29th March until 2nd November then at weekends and local school holidays during the winter. Trains run at varying times from 10.30am onwards, depending on the time of the year.
Please phone (01723) 368791 or check the railway's web site for further details.
Steam Working: None
Prices: Adult Return £3.30 (Single £2.70)
          Child Return £2.60 (Single £2.10)

E-mail: gm@nbr.org.uk

Detailed Directions by Car:
From All Parts: Take the A64, A165 or A170 to Scarborough and follow the signs for North Bay Leisure Park. The railway is situated just off the A165 opposite Peasholm Park. Alternatively, follow signs for the Sea Life Centre for Scalby Mills Station.

OLD KILN LIGHT RAILWAY

Address: Rural Life Centre, Reeds Road, Tilford, Farnham, Surrey GU10 2DL	**Nº of Steam Locos:** 2
Telephone Nº: (01252) 795571	**Nº of Other Locos:** 10
Year Formed: 1975	**Nº of Members:** 14
Location: 3 miles south of Farnham	**Annual Membership Fee:** £25.00
Length of Line: ¾ mile **Gauge:** 2 feet	**Approx Nº of Visitors P.A.:** 21,000
	Web site: www.oldkilnlightrailway.com

GENERAL INFORMATION

Nearest Mainline Station: Farnham (4 miles)
Nearest Bus Station: Farnham
Car Parking: Free parking available on site
Coach Parking: Free parking available on site
Souvenir Shop(s): Yes
Food & Drinks: Available

SPECIAL INFORMATION

The Railway is part of the Rural Life Centre at Tilford. The Centre contains the biggest country life collection in the South of England with a wide range of attractions. A line extension to ¾ mile has recently been opened.

OPERATING INFORMATION

Opening Times: 2014 dates: The Rural Life Centre is open Wednesday to Sunday and Bank Holidays from March to October, 10.00am to 5.00pm. Open Wednesdays and Sundays only during the winter from 11.00am to 4.00pm.
Steam Working: During Special Events only. 2014 dates: 19th April, 10th, 11th, 25th & 31st May, 1st June, 28th July, 30th & 31st August, 7th & 21st September.
Also Santa Specials in December. Please contact the railway for further information about all these events.
Prices: Steam-hauled rides £1.50
         Diesel-hauled rides £1.00

Detailed Directions by Car:
The Rural Life Centre is situated 3 miles south of Farnham. From Farnham take the A287 southwards before turning left at Millbridge crossroads into Reeds Road. The Centre is on the left after about ½ mile, just after the Frensham Garden Centre; From the A3: Turn off at the Hindhead crossroads and head north to Tilford. Pass through Tilford, cross the River Wey then turn left into Reeds Road. The Centre is on the right after ½ mile.

PERRYGROVE RAILWAY

Address: Perrygrove Railway, Coleford, Gloucestershire   GL16 8QB
Telephone Nº: (01594) 834991
Year Formed: 1996
Location of Line: ½ mile south of Coleford
Length of Line: ¾ mile

Nº of Steam Locos: 4
Nº of Other Locos: 3
Nº of Members: 6
Approx Nº of Visitors P.A.: 20,000
Gauge: 15 inches
Web site: www.perrygrove.co.uk

GENERAL INFORMATION

Nearest Mainline Station: Lydney (for Parkend)
Nearest Bus Station: Bus stops in Coleford
Car Parking: Free parking available on site
Coach Parking: Free parking on site
Souvenir Shop(s): Yes
Food & Drinks: Sandwiches & light refreshments are available

SPECIAL INFORMATION

Perrygrove is a unique railway with 4 stations, all with access to private woodland walks. Lots of picnic tables are available in the open and under cover. There is also an indoor village with secret passages, a play area and an exciting Treetop Adventure accessible to all.

OPERATING INFORMATION

Opening Times: Every Saturday, Sunday and Bank Holiday and daily throughout the local school holidays. Santa Specials also run (pre-booking is essential for these). Please phone for further details. Railway opens at 10.30am with the last train time depending on the time of year.
Steam Working: Most services are steam-hauled and driver experience courses are also available.
Prices: Adult £6.30 (All-day ticket)
  Senior Citizen £5.80 (All-day ticket)
  Child (ages 3-16) £4.90 (All-day ticket)

Detailed Directions by Car:
From All Parts: Travel to Coleford, Gloucestershire. Upon reaching the vicinity of Coleford, the Perrygrove Railway is clearly signposted with brown tourist signs from all directions.   SATNAVs use this post code: GU16 8QB

Ravenglass & Eskdale Railway

Address: Ravenglass, Cumbria
CA18 1SW
Telephone Nº: (01229) 717171
Year Formed: 1875
Location: The Lake District National Park
Length of Line: 7 miles

Gauge: 15 inches
Nº of Steam Locos: 6
Nº of Other Locos: 8
Nº of Members: None
Approx Nº of Visitors P.A.: 120,000
Web site: www.ravenglass-railway.co.uk
E-mail: steam@ravenglass-railway.co.uk

GENERAL INFORMATION

Nearest Mainline Station: Ravenglass (adjacent)
Nearest Bus Stop: Ravenglass
Car Parking: Available at both terminals
Coach Parking: At Ravenglass
Souvenir Shop(s): Yes
Food & Drinks: Yes

SPECIAL INFORMATION

From Ravenglass, the Lake District's only coastal village, the line runs through two lovely valleys to the foot of England's highest mountain. A new station and visitor centre featuring Fellbites eatery, Scafell Gift Shop and the Eskdale Meeting Room is now open at Dalegarth (Eskdale).

OPERATING INFORMATION

Opening Times: 2014 dates: The service runs daily from 15th March until the 2nd November inclusive. Trains also run during most weekends in the Winter, daily during February half-term and Santa Specials operate on other dates in December and early January. Open from 9.00am to 5.00pm (sometimes later during high season).
Steam Working: Most services are steam hauled.
Prices: Adult £13.00
Child £6.50 (Ages 5 to 15)
Under-5s travel free
Family Ticket £35.00
(Unlimited travel for 2 adults + 2 children)

Detailed Directions by Car:
The railway is situated just off the main A595 Western Lake District road.

RHIW VALLEY LIGHT RAILWAY

Address: Lower House Farm, Manafon, Nr. Welshpool SY21 8BJ	**N° of Steam Locos**: 2
Telephone N°: None	**N° of Other Locos**: 1
Year Formed: 1971	**Approx N° of Visitors P.A.**: 1,000
Location of Line: By the side of the B4390 between Berriew and Manafon	**Gauge**: 15 inches
	Web site: www.rvlr.co.uk
Length of Line: ¾ mile	**E-mail**: steam@rvlr.co.uk

GENERAL INFORMATION

Nearest Mainline Station: Welshpool (5 miles)
Nearest Bus Station: Welshpool (5 miles)
Car Parking: Available on site
Coach Parking: Available on site
Souvenir Shop(s): None
Food & Drinks: Available during operating days

SPECIAL INFORMATION

The Rhiw Valley Light Railway is planning projects to both extend the track and also construct a new waiting room.

OPERATING INFORMATION

Opening Times: 2014 operating dates:
19th & 20th April; 3rd & 4th May; 7th & 8th June; 5th & 6th July; 2nd, 3rd, 30th & 31st August; 20th & 21st September.
Trains run from 12.00pm to 5.00pm.
Steam Working: During all operating days.
Prices: Adult £6.00
Child £4.00 (Under-3s ride free)
Concessions £5.00
Family Tickets £20.00
(2 adults + 4 children)

Detailed Directions by Car:
Take the A483 south from Welshpool then, after 5 miles, turn right onto the B4390. Pass through Berriew and Pant-y-Ffridd and the railway is located at Lower House Farm on the outskirts of Manafon.

RHYL MINIATURE RAILWAY

Address: Marine Lake, Wellington Road, Rhyl LL18 1AQ	**Nᵒ of Steam Locos:** 5
Telephone Nᵒ: (01352) 759109	**Nᵒ of Other Locos:** 3
E-mail: info@rhylminiaturerailway.co.uk	**Nᵒ of Members:** Approximately 80
Year Formed: 1911	**Annual Membership Fee:** £8.00
Location of Line: Rhyl	**Approx Nᵒ of Visitors P.A.:** 17,000
Length of Line: 1 mile	**Gauge:** 15 inches
	Web site: www.rhylminiaturerailway.co.uk

GENERAL INFORMATION

Nearest Mainline Station: Rhyl (1 mile)
Nearest Bus Station: Rhyl (1 mile)
Car Parking: Car Park near the Railway
Coach Parking: Available nearby
Souvenir Shop(s): Yes
Food & Drinks: Available

SPECIAL INFORMATION

The trust operates the oldest Miniature Railway in the UK. The principal locomotive and train have been operating there since the 1920's.

OPERATING INFORMATION

Opening Times: Every weekend from Easter until the end of September. Also on Bank Holiday Mondays, Fridays during June and July and daily during the School Summer Holidays. Trains run from 11.00am to 4.00pm.
Steam Working: Every Sunday and also Friday to Saturday during the School Summer Holidays.
Prices: Adult £2.50
       Child £1.50

Detailed Directions by Car:
From All Parts: The Railway is located behind the west end of Rhyl Promenade.

ROMNEY, HYTHE & DYMCHURCH RAILWAY

Address: New Romney Station, New Romney, Kent TN28 8PL
Telephone Nº: (01797) 362353
Year Formed: 1927
Location of Line: Approximately 5 miles west of Folkestone
Length of Line: 13½ miles

Nº of Steam Locos: 11
Nº of Other Locos: 5
Nº of Members: 2,500
Annual Membership Fee: Supporters association – Adult £19.00; Junior £8.00
Approx Nº of Visitors P.A.: 160,000
Gauge: 15 inches
Web site: www.rhdr.org.uk

GENERAL INFORMATION

Nearest Mainline Station: Folkestone Central (5 miles) or Rye
Nearest Bus Station: Folkestone (then take bus to Hythe)
Car Parking: Free parking at all major stations
Coach Parking: At New Romney & Dungeness
Souvenir Shop(s): Yes – 4 at various stations
Food & Drinks: 2 Cafes serving food and drinks plus a tea shop at Hythe Station.

SPECIAL INFORMATION

Opened in 1927 as 'The World's Smallest Public Railway'. Now the only 15" gauge tourist main line railway in the world. Double track, 7 stations.

OPERATING INFORMATION

Opening Times: 2014 dates: A daily service runs from 22nd March to 2nd November. Open at weekends in February, March and for Santa Specials during December. Also open daily during School half-terms.
Steam Working: All operational days.
Prices: Vary depending on length of journey.
Adult Day Rover £16.00
Child Day Rover £8.00
Concessionary Day Rover £14.00
Family Day Rover £43.50
(2 adults + 3 children)

Detailed Directions by Car:
Exit the M20 at Junction 11 then follow signs to Hythe and the brown tourist signs for the railway. Alternatively, Take the A259 to New Romney and follow the brown tourist signs for the railway.

ROYAL VICTORIA RAILWAY

Address: Royal Victoria Country Park, Netley, Southampton   SO31 5GA
Telephone Nº: (023) 8045-6246
Year Formed: 1995
Location of Line: Netley
Length of Line: 1 mile

Nº of Steam Locos: 6
Nº of Other Locos: 5
Approx Nº of Visitors P.A.: Not known
Gauge: 10¼ inches
Web site: www.royalvictoriarailway.co.uk

GENERAL INFORMATION

Nearest Mainline Station: Netley
Nearest Bus Station: Southampton
Car Parking: Available on site – £3.00 fee
Coach Parking: Free parking available on site
Souvenir Shop(s): Yes
Food & Drinks: Yes

SPECIAL INFORMATION

The railway runs through the grounds of an old Victorian hospital and has good views of the Solent and the Isle of Wight. The Park covers 200 acres including woodland, grassland, beaches, picnic sites and a play area.

OPERATING INFORMATION

Opening Times: Weekends throughout the year and daily during local school holidays. Trains run from 11.00am to 4.30pm. The railway also opens by appointment for larger parties.
Steam Working: On special event days only. Please phone for further details.
Prices: Adult Return £1.75
Child Return £1.25
Note: Special rates are available for groups of 10 or more when pre-booked. Under-2s travel free.

Detailed Directions by Car:
From All Parts: Exit the M27 at Junction 8 and follow the Brown Tourist signs for the Royal Victoria Country Park. You will reach the Park after approximately 3 miles. Do not use Sat Nav as the directions will be incorrect!

RUDYARD LAKE STEAM RAILWAY

Address: Rudyard Station, Rudyard, Near Leek, Staffordshire ST13 8PF
Telephone Nº: (01538) 306704
Year Formed: 1985
Location: Rudyard to Hunthouse Wood
Length of Line: 1½ miles

Nº of Steam Locos: 6
Nº of Other Locos: 3
Approx Nº of Visitors P.A.: 50,000
Gauge: 10¼ inches and 7¼ inches
Web site: www.rlsr.org

GENERAL INFORMATION

Nearest Mainline Station: Stoke-on-Trent (10 miles)
Nearest Bus Station: Leek
Car Parking: Free parking at Rudyard Station
Coach Parking: Free parking at Rudyard Station
Souvenir Shop(s): Yes
Food & Drinks: Yes – Cafe open at weekends from April to October

SPECIAL INFORMATION

The Railway runs along the side of the historic Rudyard Lake that gave author Rudyard Kipling his name. "Drive a Steam Train" courses can be booked or bought as a gift with vouchers valid for 12 months. A short 7¼ inch gauge railway also operates on special event days.

OPERATING INFORMATION

Opening Times: 2014 dates: Every Sunday and Bank Holiday from March to the end of November. Also open on every Saturday from 22nd March to 1st November and daily from 9th to 27th April, 27th to 31st May, 21st July to 31st August and 27th to 31st October. Also open on Wednesdays in June, July and September. Santa Specials run on 6th, 7th, 13th and 14th December and there is a Steam Gala on 20th and 21st September.
Steam Working: All trains are normally steam hauled. Trains run from 11.00am and the last train runs at 4.00pm.
Prices: Adult Return   £4.00
Child Return   £2.50
Other fares and Day Rover tickets are also available.

Detailed Directions by Car:
From All Parts: Head for Leek then follow the A523 North towards Macclesfield for 1 mile. Follow the brown tourist signs to the B5331 signposted for Rudyard for ½ mile. Pass under the Railway bridge and turn immediately left and go up the ramp to the Station car park.

RUISLIP LIDO RAILWAY

Address: Reservoir Road, Ruislip, Middlesex HA4 7TY
Telephone N°: (01895) 622595
Year Formed: 1979
Location of Line: Trains travel from Ruislip Lido to Woody Bay
Length of Line: 1¼ miles

N° of Steam Locos: 1
N° of Other Locos: 5
N° of Members: 166
Annual Membership Fee: £15.00
Approx N° of Visitors P.A.: 60,000
Gauge: 12 inches
Web site: www.ruisliplidorailway.org

GENERAL INFORMATION

Nearest Mainline Station: West Ruislip (2 miles)
Nearest Bus Station: Ruislip Underground Station
Car Parking: Free parking available at the Lido
Coach Parking: Free parking available at the Lido
Souvenir Shop(s): Yes
Food & Drinks: A Cafe is open on weekends and Bank Holidays. A Pub/Restaurant is open daily.

SPECIAL INFORMATION

The steam locomotive, 'Mad Bess' used by Ruislip Lido Railway was actually built by the members over a 12 year period!

OPERATING INFORMATION

Opening Times: 2014 dates: Daily from 5th April to 21st April then weekends and school holidays. Opening times later in the year had not been set at the time of publication so please contact the railway for further details.
Steam Working: See above.
Prices: Adult Return £3.00 (Single fare £2.00)
Child Return £2.50 (Single fare £1.50)
Family Return £9.00 (Single fare £6.00)
(2 adults + 2 children)
Note: Under-3s travel for free

Detailed Directions by Car:
From All Parts: Follow the signs from the A40 and take the A4180 through Ruislip before turning left onto the B469.

SALTBURN MINIATURE RAILWAY

Address: Valley Gardens, Saltburn	**Nº of Steam Locos:** Visiting locos only
Telephone Nº: 07813 153975	**Nº of Other Locos:** 3
Year Formed: 1947	**Nº of Members:** 12
Location of Line: Cat Nab to Forest Halt Stations, Saltburn	**Annual Membership Fee:** £1.00
	Approx Nº of Visitors P.A.: 20,000
Length of Line: ¾ mile	**Gauge:** 15 inches
Web site: www.saltburn-miniature-railway.org.uk	

GENERAL INFORMATION

Nearest Mainline Station: Saltburn (½ mile)
Nearest Bus Station: Saltburn (½ mile)
Car Parking: Available at Cat Nab Station
Coach Parking: Glen Side (at the top of the bank)
Souvenir Shop(s): At Cat Nab Station
Food & Drinks: None

E-mail: saltburn.miniaturerailway@ntlworld.com

OPERATING INFORMATION

Opening Times: Weekends and Bank Holidays from Easter until the end of September. Also open Tuesday to Friday during the Summer School Holidays. All services operate weather permitting. Trains run from 1.00pm to 5.00pm.
Steam Working: Please contact the railway for details.
Prices: Adult Return £2.00 (Adult Single £1.00)
Child Return 1.00 (Child Single 50p)
Note: Family tickets and frequent user discounts are also available. Under-5s ride free of charge.

Detailed Directions by Car:
Follow the A174 from Middlesbrough (West) or Whitby (East) to Saltburn-by-the-Sea. Cat Nab Station with its adjoining car park is situated by the beach, directly off the C74 (C174).

SHERWOOD FOREST RAILWAY

Address: Gorsethorpe Lane, Edwinstowe, Mansfield NG21 9HL	**N° of Steam Locos:** 2
Telephone N°: (01623) 515339	**N° of Other Locos:** 3
Year Formed: 1999	**N° of Members:** 13
Location of Line: Between Mansfield Woodhouse and Edwinstowe	**Approx N° of Visitors P.A.:** 5,000
Length of Line: 680 yards	**Gauge:** 15 inches
	Website: www.sherwoodforestrailway.com

GENERAL INFORMATION

Nearest Mainline Station: Mansfield (7 miles)
Nearest Bus Station: Mansfield (7 miles)
Car Parking: Free parking available on site
Coach Parking: Available on site
Souvenir Shop(s): Yes
Food & Drinks: Available

SPECIAL INFORMATION

The Railway runs through the grounds of Shaw-Browne Estates which has play areas for children and picnic areas. Check out the web site for up-to-date news.

OPERATING INFORMATION

Opening Times: 2014 dates: Weekends, Tuesdays and Bank Holidays from the first weekend in March until the first weekend in December. Open daily during the school holidays. Trains run from 11.00am to 4.30pm on most days.
Steam Working: Every operating day
Prices: Adults £1.50
Chidren £1.50

Detailed Directions by Car:
From the A1: Turn off at the Worksop roundabout and head to Ollerton. Follow the A6075 through Edwinstowe and towards Mansfield Woodhouse, then turn left at the double mini-roundabout. The Farm Park is on the right after approximately 200 yards; From Nottingham: Head to Ollerton, then as above; From the M1: Exit at Junction 27 and head into Mansfield. Follow signs to Mansfield Woodhouse and then on towards Edwinstowe. From here, follow the tourist signs for the Steam Railway.

SITTINGBOURNE & KEMSLEY LIGHT RAILWAY

Address: P.O. Box 300, Sittingbourne, Kent ME10 2DZ
Info/Talking Timetable: (01795) 424899
Year Formed: 1969
Location of Line: North of Sittingbourne
Length of Line: 2 miles

Nº of Steam Locos: 9 (2 Standard gauge)
Nº of Other Locos: 3
Nº of Members: 300
Annual Membership Fee: £18.00
Approx Nº of Visitors P.A.: 6,000
Gauge: 2 feet 6 inches
Web site: www.sklr.net

GENERAL INFORMATION

Nearest Mainline Station:
Sittingbourne (¼ mile)
Nearest Bus Station:
Sittingbourne Mainline station
Car Parking: Sittingbourne Retail Park (behind the KFC)
Coach Parking: Sittingbourne Retail Park
Souvenir Shop(s): Yes
Food & Drinks: Yes

SPECIAL INFORMATION

The railway is the only original preserved narrow gauge industrial steam railway in S.E. England (formerly the Bowaters Paper Company Railway). The railway celebrated 100 years of Steam locomotion in 2005 and the line includes a trip along a ½ mile concrete viaduct. Other attractions include a Museum, Model Railways, a Children's play area and a Wildlife Garden.

OPERATING INFORMATION

Opening Times: Sundays and Bank Holiday weekends from April to September. Also open on Wednesdays in August and for Santa Specials on weekends in December. Phone for details of Special Events held throughout the year.
Steam Working: Trains run from 1.00pm normally, but from 11.00am on Bank Holiday weekends and Sundays in August. Last train runs at 4.00pm (except for during some special events).
Prices: Adult Return £6.00
Child Return £3.00
Senior Citizen Return £4.00
Family Return £17.00
Note: Different fares may apply on special event days.

Detailed Directions by Car:
From East or West: Take the M2 (or M20) to A249 and travel towards Sittingbourne. Take the A2 to Sittingbourne town and continue to the roundabout outside the Mainline station. Take the turning onto the B2006 (Milton Regis) under the Mainline bridge and the car park entrance for the Railway is by the next roundabout, behind McDonalds, in the Sittingbourne Retail Park.

SNOWDON MOUNTAIN RAILWAY

Address: Llanberis, Caernarfon, Gwynedd, Wales LL55 4TY	**Length of Line:** 4¾ miles
Telephone Nº: 0844 493-8120	**Nº of Steam Locos:** 4
Fax Nº: (01286) 872518	**Nº of Other Locos:** 4
Year Formed: 1894	**Approx Nº of Visitors P.A.:** 140,000
Location of Line: Llanberis to the summit of Snowdon	**Gauge:** 2 feet 7½ inches
	Web site: www.snowdonrailway.co.uk

GENERAL INFORMATION

Nearest Mainline Station: Bangor (9 miles)
Nearest Bus Station: Caernarfon (7½ miles)
Car Parking: Llanberis Station car park – pay and display. Also other car parks nearby.
Coach Parking: As above but space is very limited
Souvenir Shop(s): Yes
Food & Drinks: Yes

SPECIAL INFORMATION

Britain's only public rack and pinion railway climbs to within 60 feet of the 3,560 feet peak of Snowdon, the highest mountain in England and Wales. The Diesel and Steam Experiences are both 2½ hour return journeys to the summit.

OPERATING INFORMATION

Opening Times: 2014 dates: Open daily (weather permitting) from 15th March until 2nd November. Trains depart at regular intervals from 9.00am. The last departure can be as late as 5.00pm depending on demand. It is advisable to guarantee tickets and book in advance either on-line or by telephone.
Steam Working: Ride the "Snowdon Lily" as part of the Heritage Steam Experience operating from May to September. Please contact the railway for further details.
Prices: Adult Summit Return £27.00 (Diesel)
Adult Summit Return £35.00 (Steam)
Child Summit Return £18.00 (Diesel)
Child Summit Return £25.00 (Steam)
Special rates are available for large groups. Please phone 0844 493-8120 for further details.

Detailed Directions by Car:
Llanberis Station is situated on the A4086 Caernarfon to Capel Curig road, 7½ miles from Caernarfon. Convenient access via the main North Wales coast road (A55). Exit at the A55/A5 junction and follow signs to Llanberis via B4366, B4547 and A4086.

SOUTH DOWNS LIGHT RAILWAY

Address: South Downs Light Railway, Stopham Road, Pulborough RH20 1DS	**Nº of Steam Locos**: 8
Telephone Nº: 07518 753784	**Nº of Other Locos**: 2
Year Formed: 1999	**Nº of Members**: 60
Location: Pulborough Garden Centre	**Annual Membership Fee**: Adult £20.00
Length of Line: 1 kilometre	**Approx Nº of Visitors P.A.**: 15,000
	Gauge: 10¼ inches
	Web site: www.south-downs-railway.com

GENERAL INFORMATION

Nearest Mainline Station: Pulborough (½ mile)
Nearest Bus Station: Bus stop just outside Centre
Car Parking: Free parking on site
Coach Parking: Free parking on site
Souvenir Shop(s): Yes
Food & Drinks: Yes – in the Garden Restaurant

SPECIAL INFORMATION

The members of the Society own and operate a large collection of 10¼ inch gauge locomotives.
The Railway is located within the Pulborough Garden Centre.

OPERATING INFORMATION

Opening Times: Weekends and Bank Holidays from March until September, Wednesdays in School Holidays and also Santa Specials at weekends in December. Trains run from 11.00am to 3.30pm.
Steam Working: Most services are steam hauled.
Prices: Adult £1.50
　　　　　 Child £1.00 (Under-2s travel free of charge)
Note: Supersaver tickets are also available and a special 'South Downs Belle' runs on the first Sunday of each month.

Detailed Directions by Car:
From All Parts: The Centre is situated on the A283, ½ mile west of Pulborough. Pulborough itself is on the A29 London to Bognor Regis Road.

SOUTHEND PIER RAILWAY

Address: Western Esplanade,
Southend-on-Sea   SS1 1EE
Telephone Nº: (01702) 618747
Year Formed: 1889
Location of Line: Southend seafront
Length of Line: 2,180 yards

Nº of Steam Locos: None
Nº of Other Locos: 2
Approx Nº of Visitors P.A.: 300,000
Gauge: 3 feet
Web site: http://www.southend.gov.uk/
info/200306/southend_pier

GENERAL INFORMATION

Nearest Mainline Station: Southend Central
(¼ mile)
Nearest Bus Station: Southend (¼ mile)
Car Parking: Available on the seafront
Coach Parking: Available
Souvenir Shop(s): Yes
Food & Drinks: Available

SPECIAL INFORMATION

The railway takes passengers to the end of Southend
Pier which, at 1.33 miles, is the longest pleasure pier
in the world.

OPERATING INFORMATION

Opening Times: Daily except for Christmas Day.
Times vary depending on the season – trains run
from 8.30am to 7.00pm during the Summer.
Steam Working: None.
Prices: Adult Return £4.00
Child Return £2.00
Concessionary Return £2.00
Family Return Ticket £10.00

Detailed Directions by Car:
From All Parts: Take the A127 to Southend and follow the brown tourist signs to the Pier.

SOUTH TYNEDALE RAILWAY

Address: The Railway Station, Alston, Cumbria CA9 3JB	**Nº of Steam Locos:** 5
Telephone Nº: (01434) 381696 (Enquiries) (01434) 382828 (Talking timetable)	**Nº of Other Locos:** 4
Year Formed: 1973	**Nº of Members:** 290
Location of Line: From Alston, northwards along South Tyne Valley to Lintley	**Annual Membership Fee:** £16.00
Length of Line: 3½ miles	**Approx Nº of Visitors P.A.:** 22,000
	Gauge: 2 feet
	Web: www.south-tynedale-railway.org.uk

GENERAL INFORMATION

Nearest Mainline Station: Haltwhistle (15 miles)
Nearest Bus Station: Alston Townfoot (¼ mile)
Car Parking: Free parking at Alston Station but limited spaces available at Lintley Station
Coach Parking: Free parking at Alston Station but a coach drop off point only at Lintley Station
Souvenir Shop(s): Yes
Food & Drinks: A Cafe is now open at Alston Station and a buffet car runs on most services

SPECIAL INFORMATION

The railway operates along part of the old Alston to Haltwhistle branch line. An extension to Lintley opened in 2012 and the railway plans to open a further extension to Slaggyford in the future.

OPERATING INFORMATION

Opening Times: 2014 dates: Bank Holidays, weekends and School Holidays from 5th April until the 9th November. Open daily from 19th July to 31st August (closed on Fridays). Also open Tuesdays and Thursdays and other dates in June. Santa Specials will operate in December. Please contact the Railway for further details.
Steam Working: Generally most weekends and Bank Holidays plus some other dates and Santa Specials during December.
Prices: Adult Return £10.00;   Adult Single £5.00
  Child Return £4.00;   Child Single £2.00
  Family Return Ticket £24.00
    (2 Adults + 3 Children)
  Children under 3 travel free

Detailed Directions by Car:
Alston can be reached by a number of roads from various directions including A689, A686 and the B6277. Alston Station is situated just off the A686 Hexham road, north of Alston Town Centre. Look for the brown tourist signs on roads into Alston.   Lintley Station is signposted off the A689.

STEEPLE GRANGE LIGHT RAILWAY

Address: High Peak Trail, Near National Stone Centre, Wirksworth   DE4 4LS
Telephone Nº: (01629) 580917
Operating Day Contact Nº: 07769 802587
Year Formed: 1986
Location of Line: Off the High Peak trail near Wirksworth
Length of Line: ½ mile at present

Nº of Steam Locos: None at present
Nº of Other Locos: 16
Nº of Members: 200
Annual Membership Fee: From £8.00
Approx Nº of Visitors P.A.: 8,000+
Gauge: 18 inches
Web site: www.steeplegrange.co.uk

GENERAL INFORMATION

Nearest Mainline Station: Cromford (2 miles)
Nearest Bus Station: Matlock
Car Parking: Available nearby
Coach Parking: Available nearby
Souvenir Shop(s): Yes
Food & Drinks: Light refreshments available

SPECIAL INFORMATION

The Railway is built on the track bed of the former Standard Gauge Cromford and High Peak Railway branch to Middleton. The railway uses mostly former mining/quarrying rolling stock and has two separate lines operating.

OPERATING INFORMATION

Opening Times: Sundays and Bank Holidays from Easter until the end of October. Also open on Saturdays in July and August and on other days by prior arrangement. Special Events at other times of the year including Santa Specials during December. Please contact the railway for further information. Trains run from 12.00pm to 5.00pm
Steam Working: None at present
Prices: Adult Return £3.00   Child Return £1.50
Senior Citizen Return £2.00
Family Return £8.00
Note: Special fares apply during special events and also for group bookings.

Detailed Directions by Car:
The Railway is situated adjacent to the National Stone Centre just to the north of Wirksworth at the junction of the B5035 and B5036. Car parking is available at the National Stone Centre and in Old Porter Lane.

SUTTON HALL RAILWAY

Address: Tabors Farm, Sutton Hall, Shopland Road, near Rochford, Essex SS4 1LQ	**No of Steam Locos**: 1
Telephone No: (01702) 334337	**No of Other Locos**: 1
Year Formed: 1997	**No of Members**: Approximately 8
Location of Line: Sutton Hall Farm	**Annual Membership Fee**: £15.00
Length of Line: Almost 1 mile	**Approx No of Visitors P.A.**: 3,500
	Gauge: 10¼ inches
	Web site: None at present

GENERAL INFORMATION

Nearest Mainline Station: Rochford (1½ miles)
Nearest Bus Station: Rochford
Car Parking: Free parking available on site
Coach Parking: Free parking available on site
Souvenir Shop(s): None
Food & Drinks: Drinks and snacks available

SPECIAL INFORMATION

The Railway was bought by C. Tabor in 1985 for use with his Farm Barn Dances. The Sutton Hall Railway Society was formed in 1997 (with C. Tabor as Society President) and now opens the line for public running on some Sundays. The railway is staffed entirely by Volunteer Members of the Society.

OPERATING INFORMATION

Opening Times: Open the 4th Sunday in the month from April until September, 12.00pm to 6.00pm. Specials run on Easter Sunday afternoon, Halloween evening (5.00pm to 10.00pm) and a Santa Special on the afternoon of the first Sunday in December (12.00pm to 5.00pm).
Steam Working: All operating days.
Prices: Adult Return £2.00
Child Return £1.50

Detailed Directions by Car:
From Southend Airport (A127 Southend to London Main Route & A1159): At the Airport Roundabout (with the McDonalds on the left) go over the railway bridge signposted for Rochford. At the 1st roundabout turn right (Ann Boleyn Pub on the right) into Sutton Road. Continue straight on at the mini-roundabout then when the road forks turn left into Shopland Road signposted for Barling and Great Wakering. Turn right after approximately 400 yards into the long tree-lined road for Sutton Hall Farm.

TALYLLYN RAILWAY

Address: Wharf Station, Tywyn, Gwynedd, LL36 9EY	**Nº of Steam Locos**: 6
Telephone Nº: (01654) 710472	**Nº of Other Locos**: 4
E-mail: enquiries@talyllyn.co.uk	**Nº of Members**: 3,500
Year Formed: 1865	**Annual Membership Fee**: Adult £25.00
Location of Line: Tywyn to Nant Gwernol	**Approx Nº of Visitors P.A.**: 50,000
Length of Line: 7¼ miles	**Gauge**: 2 feet 3 inches
	Web site: www.talyllyn.co.uk

GENERAL INFORMATION

Nearest Mainline Station: Tywyn (300 yards)
Nearest Bus Station: Tywyn (300 yards)
Car Parking: 100 yards away
Coach Parking: Free parking (100 yards)
Souvenir Shop(s): Yes
Food & Drinks: Yes

SPECIAL INFORMATION

Talyllyn Railway was the first preserved railway in the world – saved from closure in 1951. The railway was originally opened in 1866 to carry slate from Bryn Eglwys Quarry to Tywyn. Among the railway's attractions are a Narrow Gauge Railway Museum at the Tywyn Wharf terminus.

OPERATING INFORMATION

Opening Times: 2014 dates: Daily from 9th March to 2nd November. Also open on other selected dates in February, March, November and December including most weekends. Generally open from 10.30am to 5.00pm. Please contact the railway or check the web site for further details.
Steam Working: All services are steam-hauled.
Prices: Adult Return £14.50 (Day Rover ticket)
Senior Citizen Return £13.00
Children (ages 5-15) pay £2.00 if travelling with an adult. Otherwise, they pay half adult fare. Children under the age of 5 travel free of charge.
Single and shorter journeys are cheaper.

Detailed Directions by Car:
From the North: Take the A493 from Dolgellau into Tywyn; From the South: Take the A493 from Machynlleth to Tywyn.

TEIFI VALLEY RAILWAY

Address: Henllan Station, Henllan, near Newcastle Emlyn, Carmarthenshire	**Nº of Steam Locos**: 2
	Nº of Other Locos: 3
Telephone Nº: (01559) 371077	**Nº of Members**: Approximately 150
Year Formed: 1978	**Annual Membership Fee**: £18.00
Location of Line: Between Cardigan and Carmarthen off the A484	**Approx Nº of Visitors P.A.**: 15,000
	Gauge: 2 feet
Length of Line: 2 miles	**Web site**: www.teifivalleyrailway.org

GENERAL INFORMATION

Nearest Mainline Station: Carmarthen (10 miles)
Nearest Bus Station: Carmarthen (10 miles)
Car Parking: Spaces for 70 cars available.
Coach Parking: Spaces for 4 coaches available.
Souvenir Shop(s): Yes
Food & Drinks: Yes (snacks only)

SPECIAL INFORMATION

The Railway was formerly part of the G.W.R. but now runs on a Narrow Gauge using Quarry Engines.

OPERATING INFORMATION

Opening Times: 2014 dates: Open from Sunday to Thursday and on Bank Holidays in April, May, June July, August and September. Trains run from 11.15am to 3.00pm (or 4.45pm in August).
Steam Working: Most operating days – please phone the Railway for further details.
Prices: Adult £7.50
            Child £5.00
A 10% discount is available for parties of 10 or more.

Detailed Directions by Car:
From All Parts: The Railway is situated in the Village of Henllan between the A484 and the A475 (on the B4334) about 4 miles east of Newcastle Emlyn.

THRELKELD QUARRY RAILWAY

Address: Threlkeld Quarry & Mining Museum, Threlkeld, Near Keswick, CA12 4TT
Telephone Nº: (01768) 779747
Year Formed: 2010
Location of Line: Cumbria
Length of Line: ½ mile

Nº of Steam Locos: 1
Nº of Other Locos: 8
Nº of Members: –
Approx Nº of Visitors P.A.: 20,000
Gauge: 2 feet
Web site: www.threlkeldquarryandminingmuseum.co.uk

GENERAL INFORMATION

Nearest Mainline Station: Penrith (14 miles)
Nearest Bus Station: Keswick (5 miles)
Car Parking: Available on site
Coach Parking: Available
Souvenir Shop(s): Yes
Food & Drinks: Available

SPECIAL INFORMATION

Underground tours are available for an extra charge. Demonstration Working Weekends in conjunction with the Vintage Excavator Trust are held on the third weekend in May and September.

OPERATING INFORMATION

Opening Times: Daily from Easter to the end of October half-term. Santa Specials also run on dates in December. Please contact the Museum for details. Open from 10.00am to 5.00pm.
Steam Working: During the School Holidays and on Bank Holiday weekends. A Steam Gala is held on the last weekend in July.
Prices: Adult Museum Entry £3.00   Rides £3.00
Child Museum Entry £1.50   Rides £1.50

Detailed Directions by Car:
From All Parts: Exit the M6 at Junction 40 and take the A66 towards Keswick. Turn off onto the B5322 at Threlkeld and follow signs for the Mining Museum.

TODDINGTON NARROW GAUGE RAILWAY

Address: The Station, Toddington, Cheltenham, Gloucestershire GL54 5DT	**Nº of Steam Locos:** 4
Telephone Nº: (01242) 621405	**Nº of Other Locos:** 5
Year Formed: 1985	**Nº of Members:** Approximately 50
Location of Line: 5 miles south of Broadway, Worcestershire, near the A46	**Annual Membership Fee:** £6.00
	Approx Nº of Visitors P.A.: 2,000
Length of Line: ½ mile	**Gauge:** 2 feet
	Web site: www.toddington-narrow-gauge.co.uk

GENERAL INFORMATION

Nearest Mainline Station: Cheltenham Spa or Ashchurch

Nearest Bus Station: Cheltenham

Car Parking: Parking available at Toddington, Winchcombe & Cheltenham Racecourse Stations

Coach Parking: Parking available as above

Souvenir Shop(s): None

Food & Drinks: None at the TNGR itself but available at the adjacent GWSR site.

SPECIAL INFORMATION

The railway currently has two German-built World War One Henschel locomotive trench engines.

OPERATING INFORMATION

Opening Times: 2014 dates: 20th, 21st, 26th & 27th April; 4th, 5th, 24th, 25th & 26th May; 15th, 21st & 22nd June; 13th, 25th, 26th & 27th July; 24th & 25th August; 14th & 20th September. A Narrow Gauge gala will be held at the end of the season. Please contact the railway for details. Trains usually run from every 35 minutes from around noon.

Steam Working: Operating days as listed above.

Prices: Adults £3.00
        Children £1.00 (Under-5s ride free)

Note: Diesel only operating days are also planned on various Sundays from April to September. Please contact the railway for further details.

Detailed Directions by Car:

Toddington is 11 miles north east of Cheltenham, 5 miles south of Broadway just off the B4632 (old A46). Exit the M5 at Junction 9 towards Stow-on-the-Wold for the B4632. The Railway is clearly visible from the B4632.

VALE OF RHEIDOL RAILWAY

Address: Park Avenue, Aberystwyth, Ceredigion SY23 1PG
Telephone Nº: (01970) 625819
Year Formed: 1902
Location of Line: Aberystwyth to Devil's Bridge
Length of Line: 11¾ miles

Nº of Steam Locos: 3
Nº of Other Locos: 1
Approx Nº of Visitors P.A.: 41,000
Gauge: 1 foot 11¾ inches
Web site: www.rheidolrailway.co.uk

GENERAL INFORMATION

Nearest Mainline Station: Aberystwyth (adjacent)
Nearest Bus Station: Aberystwyth (adjacent)
Car Parking: Available on site
Coach Parking: Parking available on site
Souvenir Shop(s): Yes – At Aberystwyth
Food & Drinks: At Devil's Bridge and Aberystwyth

SPECIAL INFORMATION

The journey between the stations take one hour in each direction. At Devil's Bridge there is a cafe, toilets, a picnic area and the famous Mynach Falls. The line climbs over 600 feet in 11¾ miles. Look out for the Red Kites and Buzzards flying overhead!

OPERATING INFORMATION

Opening Times: 2014 dates: Regular services run daily from 29th March to 2nd October and on some other dates in October and November.
Santa Specials also operate on dates in December. Please check the web site or phone the railway for further information.
Steam Working: All trains are steam-hauled.
Prices: Adult Return £18.00
Senior Citizen Return £17.00
Accompanied Child Return £6.00
Unaccompanied Child Return £9.00

Detailed Directions by Car:
From the North take A487 into Aberystwyth. From the East take A470 and A44 to Aberystwyth. From the South take A487 or A485 to Aberystwyth. The Station is located in the centre of town near the 'Park and Ride' site.

VALLEY INTERNATIONAL PARK RAILWAY

Address: Valley International Park,
Crossford, Carluke   ML8 5NJ
Telephone Nº: (01555) 860150
Year Formed: 1992
Location of Line: Crossford, Lanarkshire
Length of Line: 1 mile
Nº of Steam Locos: None

Nº of Other Locos: 1
Approx Nº of Visitors P.A.: 100,000 (to
the Park itself)
Gauge: 2 feet
Web site:
www.valleyinternationalp.ipower.com

GENERAL INFORMATION

Nearest Mainline Station: Carluke (2½ miles)
Nearest Bus Station: Lanark (5 miles)
Car Parking: Available on site
Coach Parking: Available
Souvenir Shop(s): Various retail outlets at the Park
Food & Drinks: Available

SPECIAL INFORMATION

The Valley International Park is adjacent to the River
Clyde and has extensive child play facilities amongst
other attractions.

OPERATING INFORMATION

Opening Times: 2014 dates: Daily from Easter
until 26th October. Open from 10.00am to 5.00pm.
Steam Working: None
Prices: £2.00 per ride

Detailed Directions by Car:
From All Parts: Exit the M74 at Junction 7 and take the A72 towards Lanark. Turn left onto the B7056 at Crossford
then take the first turning on the right after crossing the River Clyde for access to the Park.

VOLKS ELECTRIC RAILWAY

Address: Arch 285, Madeira Drive, Brighton BN2 1EN
Telephone Nº: (01273) 292718
Year Formed: 1883
Location of Line: Brighton seafront
Length of Line: 1 mile

Nº of Steam Locos: None
Nº of Other Locos: 7
Approx Nº of Visitors P.A.: 250,000
Gauge: 2 feet 8½ inches
Web site: www.volkselectricrailway.co.uk

GENERAL INFORMATION

Nearest Mainline Station: Brighton (2 miles)
Nearest Bus Station: Brighton Pier (¼ mile)
Car Parking: Available on site
Coach Parking: Available
Souvenir Shop(s): Yes
Food & Drinks: Available

SPECIAL INFORMATION

Opened in 1883, Volk's Electric Railway is the world's oldest operating electric railway. The brainchild of inventor Magnus Volk, the railway runs for just over a mile along Brighton seafront between Aquarium (for Brighton Pier) and Black Rock (for the Marina).

OPERATING INFORMATION

Opening Times: 2014 dates: Open daily from 5th April to 30th September, usually from 10.15am to 5.00pm (11.15am starts on Tuesdays and Fridays). Services run until 6.00pm on weekends and Bank Holidays.
Steam Working: None
Prices: Adult Return £3.60 (Single £2.70)
    Child Return £2.10 (Single £1.60)
    Concessionary Return £2.70 (Single £1.80)
    Family Return £9.30 (Single £6.90)

Detailed Directions by Car:
From All Parts: Take the A23/A27 to Brighton. The railway is located on the seafront next to the Pier and Wheel.

WATERWORKS RAILWAY

Address: Kew Bridge Steam Museum, Green Dragon Lane, Brentford TW8 0EN **Telephone N°:** (020) 8568-4757 **Year Formed:** 1986 **Location of Line:** Greater London **Length of Line:** Under 1 mile	**N° of Steam Locos:** 1 **N° of Other Locos:** 1 **N° of Members:** 750 **Annual Membership Fee:** £20.00 Adult **Approx N° of Visitors P.A.:** 20,000 **Gauge:** 2 feet **Web site:** www.kbsm.org

GENERAL INFORMATION

Nearest Mainline Station: Kew Bridge (3 minute walk)

Nearest Bus Station: Bus stop across the road – Services 65, 267 and 237

Car Parking: Spaces for 43 cars available on site

Coach Parking: Available on site – book in advance

Souvenir Shop(s): Yes

Food & Drinks: Yes – at weekends only

SPECIAL INFORMATION

The Museum is a former Victorian Pumping Station with a collection of working Steam Pumping Engines. The Railway demonstrates typical water board use of Railways.

OPERATING INFORMATION

Opening Times: Weekends and Bank Holidays throughout the year. Open from 11.00am to 4.00pm.

Steam Working: Sundays and Bank Holiday Mondays from April to October and also on other special event days.

Prices: Adult £10.00 (Annual tickets)
Under-16s £4.00 (Under-5s free of charge)
Senior Citizen £9.00 (Annual tickets)
Family Ticket £24.00 (2 adults + 2 children)
Family Ticket £14.00 (1 adult + 2 children)

Detailed Directions by Car:

From All Parts: Exit the M4 at Junction 2 and follow the A4 to Chiswick Roundabout. Take the exit signposted for Kew Gardens & Brentford. Go straight on at the next two sets of traffic lights following A315 towards Brentford. After 2nd set of lights take the first right for the museum. The museum is next to the tall Victorian tower.

WATFORD MINIATURE RAILWAY

Address: Cassiobury Park, Watford, WD17 7LB
Telephone Nº: 07511 749248
Year Formed: 1959
Location: At the northern end of Cassiobury Park, Watford
Length of Line: 600 yards

Nº of Steam Locos: None
Nº of Other Locos: 2
Approx Nº of Visitors P.A.: 25,000
Gauge: 10¼ inches
Web site: None

GENERAL INFORMATION

Nearest Mainline Station: Watford Junction (appoximately 1½ miles)
Nearest Tube Station: Watford (400 yards)
Car Parking: Limited spaces available at the Park.
Coach Parking: None
Souvenir Shop(s): None
Food & Drinks: Cafe available in the Park.

OPERATING INFORMATION

Opening Times: Weekends and School Holidays between 11.30pm and 5.00pm.
Steam Working: None
Prices: All fares: £1.00 per ride

Detailed Directions by Car:
Exit the M25 at Junction 19 or 20 and follow the A41 to Watford. Turn right at the Dome Roundabout heading southwards on the A412 St. Albans Road and continue through Watford Town Centre onto the A412 Rickmansworth Road. Turn right onto Cassiobury Park Avenue, following the brown information sign and continue to the end of the road for the car park.

WAVENEY VALLEY RAILWAY

Address: Bressingham Steam Museum, Bressingham, Diss, Norfolk   IP22 2AB
Telephone Nº: (01379) 686900
Year Formed: Mid 1950's
Location of Line: Bressingham, Near Diss
Length of Line: 5 miles in total (3 lines)

Nº of Steam Locos: Many Steam locos
Nº of Members: 70 volunteers
Approx Nº of Visitors P.A.: 80,000+
Gauge: Standard, 2 foot, 10¼ inches and 15 inches
Web site: www.bressingham.co.uk

GENERAL INFORMATION

Nearest Mainline Station: Diss (2½ miles)
Nearest Bus Station: Bressingham (1¼ miles)
Car Parking: Free parking for 400 cars available
Coach Parking: Free parking for 30 coaches
Souvenir Shop(s): Yes
Food & Drinks: Yes

SPECIAL INFORMATION

The railway operates at the Bressingham Steam Museum which, in addition to Steam locomotives, has a large selection of steam traction engines, fixed steam engines, the National Dad's Army Museum, two extensive gardens and a water garden centre.

OPERATING INFORMATION

Opening Times: 2014 dates: Daily from 1st April to 2nd November. Open from 10.30am to 5.00pm and until 5.30pm in June, July and August.
Steam Working: Almost every operating day except for most Mondays and Tuesdays in March, April, May, June, July, September and October. Please phone the Museum for further details.
Prices: Adult £11.00 (non-Steam) £13.95 (Steam)
  Child £7.25 (non-Steam) £9.95 (Steam)
  Seniors £10.00 (non-Steam) £12.50 (Steam)

Detailed Directions by Car:
From All Parts: Take the A11 to Thetford and then follow the A1066 towards Diss for Bressingham. The Museum is signposted by the brown tourist signs.

WELLS & WALSINGHAM LIGHT RAILWAY

Address: The Station, Wells-next-the-Sea
NR23 1QB
Telephone Nº: (01328) 711630
Year Formed: 1982
Location of Line: Wells-next-the-Sea to
Walsingham, Norfolk
Length of Line: 4 miles

Nº of Steam Locos: 2
Nº of Other Locos: 2
Nº of Members: 50
Annual Membership Fee: £11.00
Approx Nº of Visitors P.A.: 20,000
Gauge: 10¼ inches
Website: www.wellswalsinghamrailway.co.uk

GENERAL INFORMATION

Nearest Mainline Station: King's Lynn (21 miles)
Nearest Bus Station: Norwich (24 miles)
Car Parking: Free parking at site
Coach Parking: Free parking at site
Souvenir Shop(s): Yes
Food & Drinks: Yes

SPECIAL INFORMATION

The Railway is the longest 10¼ inch narrow-gauge steam railway in the world. The course of the railway is famous for wildlife and butterflies in season.

OPERATING INFORMATION

Opening Times: 2014 dates: Daily from 4th April until 2nd November.
Steam Working: Trains run from either 10.15am or 10.30am on most operating days.
Prices: Adult Return £9.00
Child Return £7.00

Detailed Directions by Car:
Wells-next-the-Sea is situated on the North Norfolk Coast midway between Hunstanton and Cromer. The Main Station is situated on the main A149 Stiffkey Road. Follow the brown tourist signs for the Railway.

WELSH HIGHLAND HERITAGE RAILWAY

Address: Tremadog Road, Porthmadog, Gwynedd LL49 9DY	**N° of Steam Locos:** 3
Telephone N°: (01766) 513402	**N° of Other Locos:** 18
Year Formed: 1961	**N° of Members:** 1,000
Location of Line: Opposite Porthmadog Mainline Station	**Annual Membership Fee:** £30.00 Adult
	Approx N° of Visitors P.A.: 25,000
Length of Line: 1½ mile round trip	**Gauge:** 1 foot 11½ inches
	Web site: www.whr.co.uk

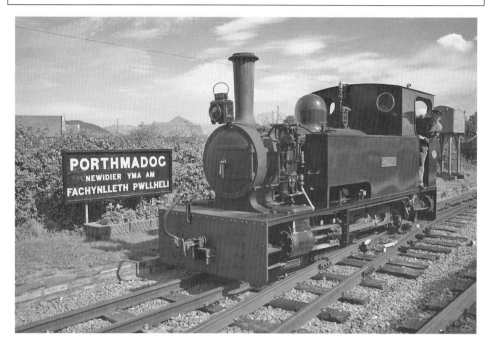

GENERAL INFORMATION

Nearest Mainline Station: Porthmadog (adjacent)
Nearest Bus Station: Services 1 & 3 stop 50 yards away
Car Parking: Free parking at site, plus a public Pay and Display car park within 100 yards
Coach Parking: Adjacent
Souvenir Shop(s): Yes – large range available
Food & Drinks: Yes – excellent home cooking at the Russell Team Room!

SPECIAL INFORMATION

The Welsh Highland Railway is a family-orientated attraction based around a Railway Heritage Centre and includes a guided, hands-on tour of the sheds.

OPERATING INFORMATION

Opening Times: 2014 dates: Daily from 5th April to 2nd November except for some Mondays and Fridays during September & October. Trains run at 10.30am, 11.30am, 1.00pm, 2.00pm, 3.00pm and 4.00pm (the last train runs at 3.00pm during October and November).
Steam Working: Daily during the School Holidays and on other selected weekends. Please check with the railway for further details.
Prices: Adult Day Rover £7.50
Child Day Rover £3.75 (Under-5s free)
Senior Citizen Day Rover £6.00
Family Day Rover £18.50
(2 adults + 2 children)

Detailed Directions by Car:
From Bangor/Caernarfon take the A487 to Porthmadog. From Pwllheli take the A497 to Porthmadog then turn left at the roundabout. From the Midlands take A487 to Portmadog. Once in Porthmadog, follow the brown tourist signs. The line is located right next to Porthmadog Mainline Station, opposite the Queens Hotel.

WELSH HIGHLAND RAILWAY

Postal Address: Ffestiniog Railway, Harbour Station, Porthmadog LL49 9NF	**Nº of Steam Locos:** 8 (5 working)
Telephone Nº: (01766) 516000	**Nº of Other Locos:** 3
Year Formed: 1997	**Nº of Members:** 2,300
Location: Caernarfon to Porthmadog	**Annual Membership Fee:** £23.00
Length of Line: 25 miles	**Approx Nº of Visitors P.A.:** 360,000
Web site: www.festrail.co.uk	**Gauge:** 1 foot 11½ inches
	E-mail: enquiries@festrail.co.uk

GENERAL INFO

Nearest Mainline Station:
Porthmadog (½ mile) or Bangor (7 miles)
(Bus service Nº 5 to Caernarfon)
Nearest Bus Station:
Porthmadog or Caernarfon
Car Parking:
Parking available at Caernarfon
Coach Parking:
At Victoria Docks (¼ mile from Caernarfon station) and in Porthmadog
Souvenir Shop(s): Yes
Food & Drinks:
Full buffet available on most trains

SPECIAL INFO

The Railway has been reconstructed between Caernarfon and Porthmadog along the track bed of the original Welsh Highland Railway. 2011 saw the completion of this spectacular route passing from coast to coast through the majestic scenery of the Snowdonia National Park.

OPERATING INFO

Opening Times: 2014 dates: Regular services run from 25th March to 1st November. There is also a limited service in the Winter and Santa Specials on weekends in December. Train times vary depending on the date. Please contact the railway for further details.
Steam Working:
Most trains are steam-hauled.
Prices: Adult £35.00
(All-day Rover ticket)
Concessions £31.50
(All-day Rover ticket)
One child travels free with each adult, additional children travel for half the fare. Concessionary prices are available for Senior Citizens and groups of 20 or more and cheaper fares are available for single rides and shorter journeys.

Detailed Directions by Car:
Take either the A487(T), the A4085 or the A4086 to Caernarfon then follow the brown tourist signs for the Railway which is situated in St. Helens Road next to the Castle.

Welshpool & Llanfair Light Railway

Address: The Station, Llanfair Caereinion, Powys SY21 0SF
Telephone N°: (01938) 810441
Year Formed: 1959
Location of Line: Welshpool to Llanfair Caereinion, Mid Wales
Length of Line: 8 miles

N° of Steam Locos: 9
N° of Other Locos: 5
N° of Members: 2,200
Annual Membership Fee: £35.00
Approx N° of Visitors P.A.: 26,000
Gauge: 2 feet 6 inches
Web site: www.wllr.org.uk

GENERAL INFORMATION

Nearest Mainline Station: Welshpool (1 mile)
Nearest Bus Station: Welshpool (1 mile)
Car Parking: Free parking at Welshpool and Llanfair Caereinion
Coach Parking: As above
Souvenir Shop(s): Yes – at both ends of line
Food & Drinks: Yes – at Llanfair only

SPECIAL INFORMATION

The railway has the steepest gradient of any British railway, reaching a summit of 603 feet.

OPERATING INFORMATION

Opening Times: 2014 dates: Every weekend and Bank Holiday from 12th April to 2nd November. Daily from 15th to 24th April then daily from 24th May to 28th September. Closed on all Mondays and Fridays in June and September and most Mondays and Fridays in July. Santa Specials operate on 13th, 14th, 20th & 21sr December. Trains usually run from around 10.00am until 5.00pm.
Steam Working: All trains are steam-hauled
Prices: Adult £13.00
Senior Citizens £12.00
Under-16s £4.00 (Must be accompanied)
Children under the age of 3 travel free of charge.

Detailed Directions by Car:
Both stations are situated alongside the A458 Shrewsbury to Dolgellau road and are clearly signposted

WEST LANCASHIRE LIGHT RAILWAY

Address: Station Road, Hesketh Bank, Nr. Preston, Lancashire PR4 6SP
Telephone Nº: (01772) 815881
Year Formed: 1967
Location of Line: On former site of Alty's Brickworks, Hesketh Bank
Length of Line: ¼ mile

Nº of Steam Locos: 8
Nº of Other Locos: 24
Nº of Members: Approximately 110
Annual Membership Fee: £15.00 Adult; £20.00 Family
Approx Nº of Visitors P.A.: 14,500
Gauge: 2 feet
Web site: www.westlancs.org

GENERAL INFORMATION

Nearest Mainline Station: Rufford (4 miles)
Nearest Bus Station: Preston (7 miles)
Car Parking: Space for 50 cars at site
Coach Parking: Space for 3 coaches at site
Souvenir Shop(s): Yes
Food & Drinks: Only soft drinks & snacks

SPECIAL INFORMATION

The Railway is run by volunteers and there is a large collection of Industrial Narrow Gauge equipment.

OPERATING INFORMATION

Opening Times: 2014 dates: Sundays and Bank Holidays from April to the end of October. Santa Specials on 13th, 14th, 20th and 21st December and other Special Events are held during the year. Trains run from 11.30am to 5.00pm.
Steam Working: Trains operate on Sundays and Bank Holidays from April until the end of October.
Prices: Adult £2.50   Child £1.50
Family Tickets £6.00
Senior Citizens £2.00
Note: Different fares apply for Gala Days and Santa Specials.

Detailed Directions by Car:
Travel by the A59 from Liverpool or Preston or by the A565 from Southport to the junction of the two roads at Tarleton. From here follow signs to Hesketh Bank. The Railway is signposted.

WICKSTEED PARK RAILWAY

Address: Wicksteed Park, Kettering, NN15 6NJ	**Nº of Steam Locos**: None
Telephone Nº: 08700 621194	**Nº of Other Locos**: 3
Year Formed: 1931	**Approx Nº of Visitors P.A.**: 200,000 (visitors to Wicksteed Park)
Location of Line: Wicksteed Park	**Gauge**: 2 feet
Length of Line: 1¼ miles	**Web site**: www.wicksteedpark.co.uk

GENERAL INFORMATION

Nearest Mainline Station: Kettering (2 miles)
Nearest Bus Station: Kettering (2 miles)
Car Parking: Available on site (£6.00 entrance fee per car in the Summer, £4.00 Autumn, £2.00 Spring)
Coach Parking: Free parking available on site
Souvenir Shop(s): Yes
Food & Drinks: Available

SPECIAL INFORMATION

The Railway runs through the grounds of a large leisure complex, Wicksteed Park, which also houses many other attractions including a fairground, a rollercoaster and a log chute ride.

OPERATING INFORMATION

Opening Times: 2014 dates: Open at weekends from mid-February to November, daily during the school holidays and from 28th June to 3rd September. Open from 10.30am to 6.00pm in the Summer and until 4.30pm at other times.
Steam Working: None at present.
Prices: As a wide variety of rides are available, sheets of ride tickets can be purchased at a rate of £1.00 each or £24.00 for 30 tickets. Each trip on the railway costs 2 ride tickets. Alternatively wristbands which allow unlimited use of all attractions on the day of purchase are also available priced at £16.50 for Children, £14.00 for Adults and £9.00 for Senior Citizens. Group discounts are also available.

Detailed Directions by Car:

From the North: Exit the M1 at Junction 19 and take the A14 towards Kettering. Leave the A14 at Junction 10 and follow signs for Wicksteed Park. Alternatively take the A1 to Stamford, the A43 to Kettering then the A14 as above; From the South: Exit the M1 at Junction 15 and take the A43 to the junction with the A14, then as above. Alternatively take the A1 to the Junction with the A14 then continue to Junction 10 as above.

WINDMILL ANIMAL FARM RAILWAY

Address: Windmill Animal Farm, Red Cat Lane, Burscough L40 1UQ **Telephone Nº**: (07971) 221343 **Year Formed**: 1997 **Location of Line**: Burscough, Lancashire **Length of Line**: 1 mile	**Nº of Steam Locos**: 5 **Nº of Other Locos**: 6 **Nº of Members**: 7 **Annual Membership Fee**: None **Approx Nº of Visitors P.A.**: 40,000 **Gauge**: 15 inches **Web**: www.windmillanimalfarm.co.uk

GENERAL INFORMATION

Nearest Mainline Station: Burscough (2½ miles)
Nearest Bus Station: Southport (8½ miles)
Car Parking: Available at the Farm
Coach Parking: Available at the Farm
Souvenir Shop(s): Yes
Food & Drinks: Available

SPECIAL INFORMATION

In addition to the railway, the site includes a play area and a large number of farm animals with a petting area where children can feed the animals.

OPERATING INFORMATION

Opening Times: 2014 dates: Open Daily from Easter until November and during weekends and school holidays at all other times. Trains run from 11.00am to 4.30pm.
Steam Working: Every weekend
Prices: Adult Admission £6.00 (Farm entrance)
      Child Admission £7.00 (Farm entrance)
      Senior Citizen Admission £4.50 (Farm ent.)
      Family Admission £24.00 (Farm entrance)
Train Rides: Adult £1.50
      Child £1.00 (Under-2s ride free)

Detailed Directions by Car:
From All Parts: Exit the M6 at Junction 27 and take the A5209 following signs for Southport. On entering Burscough follow signs for Burscough Bridge and Martin Lane. Turn left into Red Cat Lane just by Burscough Bridge train station and follow the road along for Windmill Animal Farm and the Railway.

WOODHORN NARROW GAUGE RAILWAY

Address: Woodhorn Northumberland
Museum, Queen Elizabeth II Country Park,
Ashington   NE63 9YF
Telephone Nº: 0790 600-9569
Year Formed: 1995
Location of Line: Northumberland
Length of Line: 1,000 yards

Nº of Steam Locos: None
Nº of Other Locos: 3
Approx Nº of Visitors P.A.: 100,000
(to the museum); 25,000 (to the railway)
Gauge: 2 feet
Web site:
woodhornnarrowgaugerailway.weebly.com

GENERAL INFORMATION

Nearest Mainline Station: Morpeth (8 miles)
Nearest Bus Station: Ashington (1 mile)
Car Parking: Available on site (£3.00 charge)
Coach Parking: Available
Souvenir Shop(s): Yes
Food & Drinks: Available

SPECIAL INFORMATION

The railway runs through the grounds of the
Woodhorn Museum and is operated by volunteers.
Wheelchair access is available on trains by request.

OPERATING INFORMATION

Opening Times: Weekends and Bank Holidays
throughout the year and daily during School
Holidays, weather permitting. Open from 10.00am
to 5.00pm (4.00pm during the winter months).
The last train departs at 3.30pm (at 2.30pm during
the winter).
Steam Working: None
Prices: Adults £2.00
            Children £1.00

Detailed Directions by Car:
From All Parts: Take the A1 to the A19 at Cramlington then the A189 towards Ashington and follow the brown
tourist signs for Woodhorn. (Beware of SatNav directions which may leave you on the wrong side of the local
goods railway line!)